Freight Dispatcher Training

How to Build and Run a Successful Truck Dispatching Business Without Owning a Single Truck: Turn Around Your Financial Situation From the Comfort of Your Home

Kayla Hobson

BREAKFREE PUBLICATIONS

BREAKFREE PUBLICATIONS

BreakFree Publications
34 N Franklin Ave Ste 687 #5198
Pinedale, WY 82941
www.breakfreepublications.com

© Copyright 2022 Ask the Sages LLC- All rights reserved.

The content contained within this book may not be reproduced, duplicated or transmitted without direct written permission from the author or the publisher.

Under no circumstances will any blame or legal responsibility be held against the publisher, or author, for any damages, reparation, or monetary loss due to the information contained within this book. Either directly or indirectly. You are responsible for your own choices, actions, and results.

Legal Notice: This book is copyright protected. This book is only for personal use. You cannot amend, distribute, sell, use, quote or paraphrase any part, or the content within this book, without the consent of the author or publisher.

Disclaimer Notice: Please note the information contained within this document is for educational and entertainment purposes only. All effort has been executed to present accurate, up to date, and reliable, complete information. No warranties of any kind are declared or implied. Readers acknowledge that the author is not engaging in the rendering of legal, financial, medical or professional advice. The content within this book has been derived from various sources. Please consult a licensed professional before attempting any techniques outlined in this book.

By reading this document, the reader agrees that under no circumstances is the author responsible for any losses, direct or indirect, which are incurred as a result of the use of the information contained within this document, including, but not limited to, — errors, omissions, or inaccuracies.

TABLE OF CONTENTS

Introduction   1

How to get the most out of this book   9

CHAPTER 1
Understanding the Basics of Truck Dispatching

Getting Acquainted with the Trucking Industry 16
Factoring Companies 19
What Is a Supply Chain? 20
What Does a Dispatcher Do and Why Are They Important?............... 22
Truck Dispatcher Skills and Services 24
Truck Dispatcher Vs. Freight Broker.. 26
How Much Money Can You Make as an Independent Dispatcher? 28
Is Truck Dispatching a Hard or Stressful Job? 29
Getting Started with Freight Dispatching...................................... 32
Key Takeaway... 33

CHAPTER 2
How to Start Your Dispatching Business Immediately

Essential Things You Need to Know 36
Working Remotely as a Truck Dispatcher...................................... 36
Can You Work as a Dispatcher Part-Time? 37
How Much Does It Cost to Start as an Independent Truck Dispatcher? 38
What Exactly Do You Need?.. 39
   1. Business Setup 40

    2. Compliance—Legalities of Dispatching Business 41

    3. Address and Phone 42

    4. Home Office Setup 43

    5. Marketing Plan 45

    6. Load Boards 47

Technical Terms and Industry Jargon 47

    1. General Terms 47

    2. Carrier Searches 48

    3. Load Boards 49

    4. Dialogue with Brokers or Shippers 51

    5. Invoicing and Payments 54

    6. Equipment Types 55

Key Takeaway 56

CHAPTER 3

Getting Your First Carrier

Common Equipment Types 57

    1. Reefer Trucks 59

    2. Dry Van Trailers 61

    3. Flatbed Trucks 63

    4. Power-Only Trucks 66

    5. Other Equipment Trucks 67

Finding Your First Carrier under Five Minutes 69

Dispatcher Carrier Agreement to Send Carriers 72

    1. Dispatcher Service Agreement 72

    2. Carrier Profile 73

    3. Limited Power of Attorney 74

    4. Other Documents Needed from the Carrier 75

Key Takeaway 77

CHAPTER 4

Finding Loads

What Are Load Boards?... 80
    1. Free Load Boards 80
    2. Subscription-Based Load Boards 81
Before You Go to Load Boards 84
    1. The Driver's Location 85
    2. The Driver's HOS 85
    3. Driver's Availability 86
    4. Equipment & Dispatch Details...................................... 87
How to Search The Loads 88
    1. Trip Planning... 89
    2. Weather conditions 90
    3. Traffic and time estimates... 90
    4. Market conditions.. 91
    5. Difficult areas, scales, and tolls..................................... 92
    6. TriHaul vs. Backhaul 94
Qualifying Process of Brokers.. 96
Before You Start Negotiating Rates with Brokers 99
Accessorial & Carrier Fees 101
Your Fee As A Dispatcher... 103
Calling Brokers & Rate Negotiation 104
Load Board Video Tutorial w/ Live Examples 105
What Is a Carrier Packet?... 106
Key Takeaway... 111

CHAPTER 5

Tracking Loads and Final Workflow

Typical Day of a Truck Dispatcher... 113

Daily Goals and Challenges to Expect 114
Support You Need to Give.. 114
Tracking Your Loads and Carriers... 115
    1. Using Software 115
    2. Using Spreadsheets.. 116
Understand Billing and Invoicing the Right Way 117
Workflow of Dispatching 120
Key Takeaway... 124

CHAPTER 6

Scaling Your Business

Building Your Brand.. 126
Have a Mind Shift from Solo Player to A Business 126
Make It Easy to Choose You 127
Have an Online Presence.. 130
Different Ways of Finding A Carrier 132
    1. Online Methods of Finding a Carrier 132
    2. Offline Methods of Finding a Carrier................................ 135
Scripts to Use When Calling Carriers.. 139
How to Keep Your Carriers 140
Key Takeaway... 142

Conclusion   **143**

References   **145**

Introduction

"It's your reaction to adversity, not adversity itself, that determines how your life's story will develop."

— Dieter F. Uchtdorf

THE COVID-19 PANDEMIC caused an economic bubble and recession that devastated many people worldwide. According to a joint report by the ILO, FAO, IFAD, and WHO, the pandemic disrupted economic and social activities, resulting in tens of millions of people becoming extremely poor. In addition, the number of undernourished people was estimated at nearly 132 million in late 2019 but then grew to 690 million by the end of 2020.

Sadly, our financial future and security have never been in greater danger than now. You may have guessed this much from the recent decline in the financial market, the number of companies going bankrupt, and the huge losses many businesses have suffered since the pandemic.

Maybe you even lost your job during the pandemic and are still unemployed. Worse yet, with how the stock market is going, things don't seem like they might improve anytime soon. In fact, financial experts predict the U.S. will suffer an even worse recession if the government doesn't intervene soon. Unfortunately, while you're waiting on the government for a solution, every new day presents you with more problems, like outstanding debts, increased rent, and insufficient funds.

At this point, isn't it high time you did something to improve your financial situation?

If you genuinely want to change your life, you need to take action now. Better yet, you need to seek better income opportunities to feed your family, pay your bills, and save money without breaking a sweat.

So what if I show you some secret hacks to starting a flexible business that offers many opportunities to change your financial situation? One that you can scale and start earning a mind-blowing income?

I know what you're thinking. This all sounds too good to be true.

Perhaps, this isn't the first time you'll discover an income opportunity that promises to fix your finances and get your life back on track. Maybe you've read many books about these opportunities and applied their knowledge, but it all ended in disappointment because you were overwhelmed with too much information.

Or maybe things didn't work out because you were tricked by those self-acclaimed gurus who only sell expensive courses and one-on-one coaching that teach lessons one could easily find online.

Regardless of your experience, age, or gender, after reading this book, you'll discover how to turn your finances around with the freight dispatching business. All you need to make the most of the strategies in this book is the drive to become an entrepreneur and the discipline to put in the necessary consistent effort.

So whether you live alone, with your partner, or with your family, if you are ready to get your life back on track, comfortably buy the things you deserve, and live your dream life, then pay keen attention to every hack I share in this guide. When done right, they can transform your life into one of freedom, comfort, and flexibility.

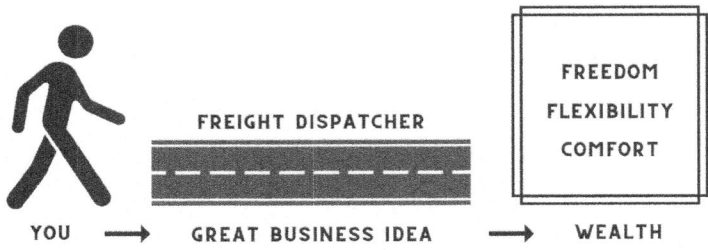

If you're a student without the time or money to go to college, and you want a flexible, lucrative business so you can attend college without collecting a student loan, then you're right on track.

I started this journey as a solopreneur and learned much about freight dispatching from the setbacks I experienced early on.

Like most people, I was laid off during the COVID-19 pandemic. The following months were hard, mainly because we had five mouths to feed (my husband, our three kids, and me). Unfortunately, my husband and I had lost nearly all our savings during the pandemic and had no emergency fund to lean back on. The financial and mental distress we experienced during this period isn't a memory I like to remember.

My youngest son, Mario, was only nine months old when I lost my job. Unfortunately, I couldn't find another full-time job despite my hard work. So I consulted employment agencies for better job offers, but they had nothing to offer me. Instead, they told me many workplaces had shut down due to the pandemic and weren't looking to hire new workers.

With no other option, I started working 10 hours a day at a grocery store in my neighborhood. After paying taxes and rent, my monthly income was only $1,834, which placed my family below the poverty line. Unfortunately, my salary wasn't enough to meet our needs, so we had no choice but to ask for help from friends and family to survive.

It was the saddest thing ever! One minute, I was happily employed and looking toward going on a vacation with my family. The next minute, I was unemployed, looking for a way for my family and me to survive those hard times.

It was indeed an overwhelming phase, and I couldn't just stand by waiting for things to fix themselves, so I set out to find a solution.

One night, after returning from the hospital where I had taken my daughter to get vaccinated, I slumped down on the couch, unlocked my phone, and browsed through YouTube videos, hoping to find something to distract me or get me to sleep.

Instead, I found a video that had me glued to my screen. It was a video by a YouTube influencer whose message was clear: **you can make thousands of dollars in your first year doing freight dispatching.**

Suddenly, I was thrilled and inspired. So I checked out this YouTube influencer's channel to be sure she knew what she was talking about, and then I found another video where she stated that she had grown her business working as a dispatcher in late 2017.

At that point, I developed a keen interest in freight dispatching. The YouTuber claimed she was financially stuck for several years but then turned her life around with the freight dispatching business. I wasn't one to trust people so quickly, but she presented herself in a way that seemed honest and reliable.

So I went back to the first video and watched it to the end, then I learned about a freight dispatching business course she had put together. But I was broke and couldn't afford it at the time.

So I saved a fraction of the little money I made doing odd jobs. And after a few weeks, I could buy the course, and she asked me to reach out to her if I needed further help. But, sadly, I hardly got any helpful info even after investing my hard-earned money and doing everything she asked me to do.

It was at that point I realized that I had been tricked. Unfortunately, most of these self-acclaimed gurus aren't who they claim to be; they simply gather information from different sources online and sell it as a course to make money. But one thing was sure—I had learned how lucrative the freight dispatch business was and gained some technical knowledge about it.

In my first three months of working as a dispatcher, I understood how difficult it was to run a business. Learning the required skills wasn't hard, but the mistakes I made as a beginner cost me hundreds of dollars and led to the early closure of my first business.

However, I didn't give up on my goals but remained focused and determined. As "luck" would have it, my second attempt sailed through, and today I have a solid understanding of the freight dispatch business and have earned a regular seven-figure income from it.

I am now passionate about teaching and empowering those who want to start a freight dispatching business but don't know how or where to start. I wrote this book to help you avoid the problems I faced when I first started, like the frustration of doing research upon research and lack of proper mentorship.

And the best part is that the tips in this book aren't just working for me; they are working wonderfully for so many others, too. Some of these people might have been in a worse situation than yours, yet they have been able to start, grow, and scale their freight dispatching business and attain financial freedom by using the strategies in this book.

Freight Dispatcher Training is a complete and detailed guide I wrote to show you how to make over $100,000 a year dispatching trucks from the comfort of your home. It is presented in a realistic yet simple style and will give you a basic understanding of the techniques involved in starting a six-figure truck dispatching business.

This book is unlike technical manuals filled with elaborate theories and formulas. It is not a *How to Get Rich Doing Freight Dispatching* book. Instead, it will help you to understand the intricacies of business, after which the "get rich doing freight dispatching" part will take care of itself.

Freight Dispatcher Training takes you beyond the rules of thumb and get-rich-quick schemes to the solid techniques used today by successful people in the freight dispatch business. After giving you a clear, concise rundown of the valuation process, this book will do the following:

- Inspire, educate, and show you how to start a remote truck dispatching business with complete confidence
- Address all the pain points and struggles that you are experiencing if you are already in the business
- Show you how to get customers (owner-operators), where to find them, and how to close the deal with them (that is, get them to sign you as their dispatcher)
- Give you a step-by-step tutorial on how and where to find loads to book for your owner-operators
- Teach you productivity hacks to help you work more efficiently as a truck dispatcher, even if you have a hectic schedule
- Guide you on how to scale your freight dispatch business and earn more money without reducing your efficiency and increasing your workload

- Answer the hundreds of questions you have about the truck dispatching business

Freight Dispatcher Training will prepare you to enter the world of freight dispatching with a giant leap forward. So whether you are a new, seasoned, or aspiring owner-operator, see this book as your roadmap to guide you through the challenges with the freight dispatch business and straight to your dream destination.

So are you ready to transform your life and take your finances to the next level?

Well, then, let's get started!

How to get the most out of this book

To help you along your freight dispatching journey, we've created a set of free bonuses that includes agreement templates, spreadsheets, bonus video content, and additional resources to help you get the best possible results.

We highly recommend download them now to get the most out of this book. You can do that by going to the link below or scanning the QR code from a scanner app.

https://ggle.io/5Qq6

Free Bonus #1 Dispatcher-to-Carrier Onboarding paperwork

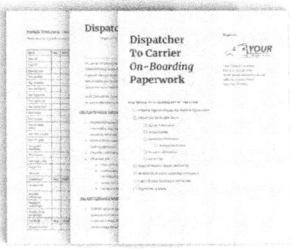

This includes the editable templates for Welcome cover, Dispatcher service agreement and complete carrier profile form.

Free Bonus #2 Invoice Templates, Credit Card Authorization Form & Fillable W-9

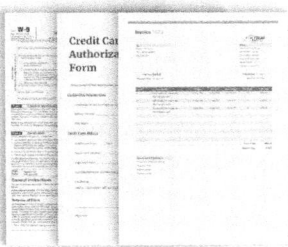

This includes two invoice templates, credit card authorization form, and fillable W9 form.

Free Bonus #3 Filled-In Samples -Know what it looks like

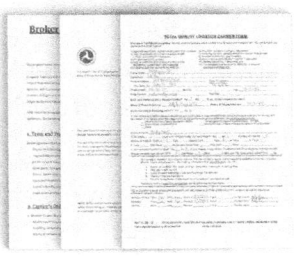

This includes real life in samples of filled in carrier packet, broker- carrier agreement, MC authority, certificate of insurance and notice of assignment.

Free Bonus #4 Freight Dispatch Load, Truck & Profit Tracker Spreadsheets

This custom spreadsheet includes a load tracker to track all your loads, a truck tracker to track all your fleet as per their running status and location, and a profit tracker to record each carrier's total gross and profit by week, month, and year.

Free Bonus #5 Three Record Keeping Sheets to Store Carrier, Driver & Broker Info

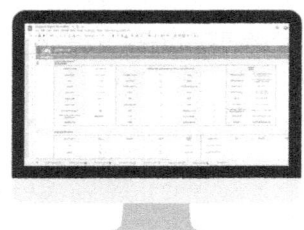

Save time and space with these info sheets for Carrier, Broker, and Driver Details. Manage all their data in one place so that you can find what you need when you need it.

Free Bonus #6 Cold Calling Management Spreadsheet

Streamline your cold calling with this custom spreadsheet, and keep track of the carrier's contact details, the dates of your contact, what they said, their status, and much more!

Free Bonus #7 Freight Dispatcher Social Media Editable Templates - 21 posts

Total 21 Social Media templates, editable in Canva. Size 1080×1080 px, Post Types include – Image, infographic, testimonial, quiz & carousel posts. Easily edit your company name, logo, colors, images, text, etc. Available with and without personal branding.

Free Bonus #8 Freight Dispatcher Logo, Trucking Logo Editable Templates - 30 Logos

Total 30 Logo templates editable in Canva with Free Subscription. Logo Styles include – Modern, Minimal, Vintage, Retro & Bling Style.

Free Bonus #9 Freight Dispatcher Flyer Templates With & Without Personal Branding

Total 6 Canva templates, including Front and Back Flyer Designs. Size A4, Orientation – Landscape. Easily edit your company name, logo, colors, images, text, etc. Available with and without personal branding.

Free Bonus #10 Freight Dispatcher Business Card Templates

Total 4 Business Card Templates, including Front and Back Designs. Size – 8.5 X 5 CM, Orientation – Landscape. Easily edit your company name, logo, colors, images, text, etc.

Free Bonus #11 Load Board Training Step by Step Video Tutorial with Live examples

Step by Step Video Tutorial on What to do before searching loads, How to use Post Trucks Feature, Search Loads Feature, Understanding Search Results, Complete Trip Planning, Analyse Market Conditions, Traffic, Tolls & Weather, Broker Credit Check, Calling Brokers, Rate Negotiation.

Free Bonus #12 Recommended Dispatcher Equipment

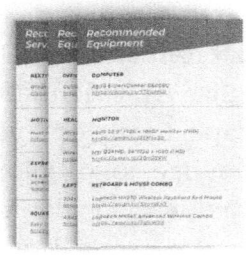

This guide includes stuff we use and recommend. A list of office equipment and services for freight dispatchers.

Free Bonus #13 Killer Script Templates

Two script templates that you can customize according to your needs. Includes My #1 Killer Script (This Script Closes 3 out of every 10 Carriers I Call!)

Free Bonus #14 Motivational Printables - 26 Posters

A set of inspirational & funny printables perfect for home office decor. Available in both Jpeg and PDF formats (Sizes A2 and A4).

We hope you enjoy your free bonuses. We put a lot of time and effort into it. To get your bonuses, go to

https://ggle.io/5Qq6

CHAPTER 1

UNDERSTANDING THE BASICS OF TRUCK DISPATCHING

"Play by the rules, but be ferocious."

— Phil Knight

ALTHOUGH BUSINESSES COME in various forms, successful ones need specific fundamental systems to thrive. These fundamental systems are the strategies used in the industry, giving the industry structure and increasing profits in the long term.

While a business may initially operate without systems, things may go wrong when it expands, adds more members to its team, or faces new challenges. However, having a system establishes control and predictability, directs priorities, fosters accountability, and provides a way for you to track your progress. But if your systems exist only in your head, you won't enjoy their full benefits because systems are easier to execute, track, and improve once programmed as strategies.

One benefit of starting a business with a working system is that you will solve your customers' problems efficiently.

After all, this is why businesses exist in the first place.

As long as problems exist, people will always look for faster, smarter, and easier solutions. So the trick to keeping your business relevant is identifying and offering effective solutions to your customers' problems. For instance, Google took online search to a whole new level, while Amazon made internet shopping and selling simpler. Likewise, Netflix found a solution for streaming movies on demand, and Uber has revolutionized the on-demand car service today.

Like the above industries, the trucking industry is one business that has a system that solves crucial problems; trust me, this is where the money is. So if you go into the trucking industry and effectively meet the market's needs, you will create a relevant, long-lasting business that will earn you so much money.

Getting Acquainted with the Trucking Industry

Before proceeding to the main context of this book, you need to understand the trucking industry and the responsibilities of its key players.

Over the years, the trucking industry has improved its

safety record dramatically. During that time, the industry has pushed for safety initiatives such as having a uniform commercial driver's license, random, mandatory drug testing, and increased roadside inspections. In the U.S., for instance, regulatory bodies continue pushing for a nationwide 65 mph speed limit.

And that's not all. New industry standards for improved logistics and the quick movement of freight mean even more opportunities. For instance, electronic data interchange, just-in-time delivery systems, and smart highway systems are growing technologies that will challenge us and require bright minds to test, develop, and expand them.

In essence, the trucking industry is not just about moving freight—it's about being a part of an increasingly sophisticated logistics system that will keep the nation's economy competitive. Here's a breakdown of how the trucking industry works, a detailed understanding of the functions of every sector, and where you can specialize in and contribute to the system:

- **Shipper:** A shipper is a person or company who is usually the owner, supplier, or manufacturer of goods or loads shipped. Also referred to as a consignor, a shipper's number one responsibility is satisfying the customer. Whatever the shipper's cargo or product is, they want it to arrive to the client promptly and intact. To achieve this goal, the shipper must find a broker to help schedule shipments with the appropriate freight carrier. The shipper must also properly and securely pack the cargo to prepare it for transportation.

- **Broker:** A broker is an intermediary between a shipper

and a carrier or trucking company; they are responsible for finding and connecting shippers and carriers. In simple terms, a shipper assigns their cargo to a broker, who puts it on a load board for different carriers to access. A load board— referred to as a freight board or a freight matching service—connects shippers and carriers. When an interested carrier finds the information on the load board, they may contact the broker to reach an agreement. Afterward, the carrier ensures the load is delivered to the consignee.

- **Carrier:** By now, you probably can tell that a carrier is a person or company that gets the load from the broker and transports it to the consignee. A carrier is a trucking company where owners manage their business with dispatchers, trailers, drivers, and other employees. Carriers are usually held responsible for any damage or loss of the items during transport. We also have the owner-operator who owns and drives their trucks and manages the business's day-to-day operations. The difference between a carrier and an owner-operator is that a carrier is either a fleet or truck company with dispatchers who can convey goods. However, owner-operators are independent contractors with the operating authority to legally deliver loads without a contract through a carrier.

- **Dispatcher:** A dispatcher is also called a fleet dispatcher, freight dispatcher, freight manager, fleet manager, logistics manager, or trucking manager. Looking at these titles, you can tell they are responsible for managing the freight. As this role is our focus throughout this guide, we will explore it in detail in subsequent sections.

Factoring Companies

Factoring companies are another key player in the trucking business. A factoring company is a third-party financing company that helps owner-operators and carriers avoid lengthy payment delays on invoices. They are not banks, although they may work with banks.

Factoring companies buy receivables from their customers, the owner-operators, or carriers at a slight discount. The client receives immediate funds from selling their receivables, providing them with the funds they need to continue running their business. The factoring company, which is now in possession of the receivables, must wait until the shippers or brokers (who sometimes handle payment processes for the shippers) pay the invoices according to their customary conditions. Like other commercial transactions, freight factoring is successful because everyone involved is motivated to participate efficiently.

Here is a detailed overview of how a factoring company functions in the trucking industry:

A shipper has prepared their cargo and needs them shipped from Location A to Location B.

The shipper, through the broker, hires an owner-operator or carrier to deliver the load. The owner-operator or carrier then prepares an invoice for the load and sends it to the shipper.

Then the owner-operator or carrier waits for thirty to forty-five days—though it could reach ninety days sometimes—before the shipper pays for the invoice; of course, this is after they must have sent the shipper a Proof of Delivery

(POD). The long waiting period is because the shippers are busy and have many shipments to make.

But then the owner-operator or carrier must act quickly as the long process time can break their business. So they turn elsewhere to meet their money needs, which is where the factoring company comes in.

The owner-operator or carrier contacts a factoring company and runs a credit check to see if the shipper's load or cargo qualifies for their service.

Once confirmed, they deliver the load and then send the invoice, the POD, and all paperwork to their factoring company.

The factoring company then purchases the invoice so the owner-operator or carrier can get paid on time.

The factoring company must now collect the payment from the shipper.

For clarification, you can think of a factoring company as health insurance. That's because owner-operators and carriers apply for the factoring services and do not just hire them without due process. The conditions of the factoring agreement will ultimately depend on the nature of this application.

What Is a Supply Chain?

A supply chain begins when the transportation industry starts its journey to the client. From the initial step of obtaining the raw materials to the final delivery of the product to end users, a supply chain is an integrated system that incorporates a sequence of procedures for creating and distributing a commodity (which may not be the final product).

The fundamental roles or sectors in a supply chain in order are as follows:

- **Raw materials shipper:** They supply manufacturers with raw materials to use in the manufacturing process.

- **Manufacturers:** The manufacturer gets those raw materials and turns them into finished products.

- **Distributors:** The manufacturer then sends the products to distribution centers for easy delivery.

- **Wholesalers:** The products leave the distribution center and get to the wholesalers or warehouses for further distribution.

- **Retailers:** The product then reaches the retailer. (Walmart is an excellent example of a retailer.)

- **Consumers:** Finally, the product is delivered to the end-user or consumer.

Looking at the supply chain process, you will agree that a broker can be involved between the raw materials shippers, manufacturers, distributors, wholesalers, retailers, and consumers. In the same way, we can have an owner-operator or carrier between each of these sectors.

Now, things get more interesting for dispatchers, as they are involved in every step of the chain—from the raw materials shippers to the consumers. So you can see that the trucking industry is a huge market with great potential to make money at any point.

What Does a Dispatcher Do and Why Are They Important?

As the backbone of the trucking industry, freight dispatchers work hard behind the scenes on a mix of support, operations, and customer service tasks to guarantee a particular consignment reaches its destination at the appointed time. Their job may look simple when you only look at the results. After all, how difficult can it be to tell a driver where their next load is?

A dispatcher might say, "Drive to Rochester, pick up 45,000 pounds of loads from XYZ Company, and deliver them to ABC in Boston by 9 a.m. on Tuesday at the latest." Unfortunately, many fail to realize the work leading to the point where the load is dispatched. Sometimes, especially with smaller operations, the dispatcher's job may overlap with other areas, such as planning, rating, and marketing.

Let's quickly explore the functions of a freight dispatcher:

- **Communicate:** As a truck dispatcher, you must talk with vendors, clients, drivers, and other logistics personnel by phone and email.

- **Coordinate:** Truck dispatchers coordinate the transportation of goods by truck with drivers, suppliers, and customers.

- **Manage:** If any issues arise along the way, such as bad weather or a vehicle maintenance problem, the truck dispatcher is responsible for informing the receiving company.

- **Negotiate:** The dispatcher acts as the middleman between a broker and the carrier. The better the dispatcher negotiates rates, the more money they make.

- **Track:** Truck dispatchers use computer systems (that this book will show you how to master) to track delivery trucks en route, ensuring that the goods arrive on time and intact.

- **Solve problems:** A dispatcher may also be required to make arrangements for repair or send a new truck to make the delivery.

Dispatchers are essential because they give carriers one less thing to worry about. So a carrier could drop off a load, scan their POW or Bill of Lading (BOL) to their dispatcher for payment, and leave for their next pickup. Carriers can dispatch their loads and cut out the middleman, but it can be time-consuming, which is why as a dispatcher, you want to make sure you are valuable to your carrier. Plus, you can offer various back-end services, which will solve even more problems for them while increasing your income with each carrier.

Truck Dispatcher Skills and Services

Dispatchers work with carriers, call and negotiate rates with brokers, get loads from the load boards, dispatch drivers to different locations, and map out their routes. They are the engine of the owner-operator and carrier business. As a dispatcher, your role is to keep portfolios of your carrier's lane preferences, desired freight rates, and equipment specifications.

Let's start by discussing the five essential skills you need to function as an independent dispatcher:

- **Computer skills:** You need to be able to use the computer to perform specific tasks such as finding loads using a load board, generating invoices, and preparing the paperwork. You will also be making calls and sending emails, so you want to ensure that you are computer savvy.

- **Analytical thinking:** This will help you during planned and unplanned situations. Trust me—there will be several unexpected situations, such as truck breakdowns, falling offloads, or loads being canceled once your drivers reach their destination. In such cases, you have to think and act fast, so your analytical skills will play a big part in your success as a dispatcher.

- **Language skills:** You should be fluent in English, too, which is a plus if you know a second language. Although I don't speak a second language currently, as I am based in the U.S. and mostly work with Americans, I hope to learn one later in life. In addition, being fluent in your language will help you communicate with brokers, owner-operators, carriers, drivers, and customers on a professional level, making them take you seriously.

- **Interpersonal skills:** This fourth skill is a big one for me. You will be working with different people with different behaviors and personalities. For instance, you will meet the nicest consignees and the rudest ones, too. But you always want to stay professional to build a good working relationship with them. This will require you to use your interpersonal skills effectively so you are not tempted to scream or shout at those who get on your nerves.

- **Industry knowledge:** This should have come first, but I saved the best for last. You need to have a good knowledge and understanding of the transportation industry and the enacted laws and regulations. This can make or break your business if you are new to dispatching.

I can guarantee that your broker or customer will not take you seriously if they feel you do not understand the trucking industry well enough. If a broker thinks you're incompetent, they might refuse to trust you with their load. So you want to make sure that you acquire the proper industry knowledge. And, of course, you will as you read through the pages of this guide.

The responsibility of a dispatcher includes ensuring that the vehicles under their supervision are loaded fairly, promptly, and economically before they are taken to where they will be unloaded and reloaded. A dispatcher usually has to work under pressure, so if you are easily irritated or anxious, you might need to work on that.

Truck Dispatcher Vs. Freight Broker

Brokers are different from dispatchers because they are the middlemen between shippers and carriers, but they usually work on behalf of shippers. Here is an illustration:

A shipper has a load and reaches out to a broker to find them a carrier. The shipper and the broker agree on a $4,000 fee. The broker then reaches out to a carrier and discusses the shipper's load with them. The broker and the carrier then agree on a $3,400 fee to haul the load. In the end, the broker keeps the $600 difference as a commission earned for a load negotiated initially for $4,000.

Negotiating one price with a shipper and a lower rate with an owner-operator is precisely how many freight brokers make their money. And since this keeps them in business, brokers put a lot of effort into supporting carriers and owner-operators.

The dispatcher is the middleman between the owner-operators or carriers, drivers, and other logistics personnel. They represent the carrier when negotiating freight. Here is another illustration for better understanding:

The shipper and the broker agree on a $4,000 fee like before. However, instead of directly working with the broker, the carrier uses a dispatcher to find freight. The dispatcher knows the carrier needs to make nothing below $3,400 on the load to stay in business and knows what each load should pay.

The dispatcher then contacts the broker about the load. The broker offers the load at $3,400, but the dispatcher declines the offer. The two negotiate until the broker agrees to a $3,600 rate. The dispatcher then contacts the carrier about the load, and the carrier agrees to haul it. The dispatcher charges the carrier a 4% fee. Ultimately, the carrier earns $3,656, the dispatcher makes $144, and the broker receives $200.

Let's do a further study to see how these two roles are different from each other:

- **Who is the customer?:** Freight brokers' customers are shippers, while freight dispatchers' customers are owner-operators and carriers.

- **What it takes to get started:** Getting started as a broker requires a lot of money. You will need an LLC, EIN, authority, and a $75,000 surety bond to get your BOC-3. But as a dispatcher, you need to form your company by getting an LLC and EIN and then get ready to hustle—that's all! As for authority, you could always use your carriers' authority to dispatch the load for them.

- **Customer acquisition:** Brokers need to do cold calling to shippers, while dispatchers need to do the same for carriers instead of shippers. Cold calling includes strategies like online marketing and advertising on offline truck events or truck stops.

- **How they get paid:** Brokers get paid by the shippers; dispatchers get paid by carriers. Most of the time, brokers and dispatchers use a factoring company to speed up the cash flow.

- **How time-consuming is their job:** Brokering takes little time, while dispatching takes much time.

How Much Money Can You Make as an Independent Dispatcher?

The earnings of freight dispatchers largely depend on the business's size and the dispatch office's tasks. Base pay is usually around $6,000 to $10,000 yearly and often more, and dispatchers with just one truck typically charge 3-8% of their fee. Using semi-trucks, for example, you can make around $240 to $640 per week and $960 to $2,560 per month. So, on average, a dispatcher will earn about $1,000 per month.

Of course, the above numbers are for semi-trucks, meaning the estimated payment will decrease if you choose a smaller vehicle. Once a new dispatcher has gathered the necessary work experience, raises tend to come quickly. Since major carriers prefer to work with seasoned professionals, most people wanting to enter the business find it easier to land their first position with a smaller company.

Once dispatchers gain experience, their skills become valuable, and their income quickly increases. Payments of $5,000 to $10,000 per month are not unusual if you have got around five to ten trucks. With that, you can dispatch for small fleet owners (more details in a later chapter).

Finding these many trucks means you will have to do marketing. But managing more than five trucks can be somewhat stressful, so you would need to outsource some tasks by hiring virtual assistants to fill broker carrier packets to save time. You could even train them to make phone calls to serve as a backup. Of course, we will go into more detail in a subsequent chapter.

Freight dispatchers can also earn money through back-end

offers. As I have explained previously, there are a lot of problems to solve in the trucking industry, and you could develop tailored solutions to solve these problems and make money in return. Trust me—some people have scaled their dispatch business to more than 100K monthly revenue. So you see, the possibilities are endless.

Is Truck Dispatching a Hard or Stressful Job?

Although your potential income is essential in deciding if freight dispatching is the right option for you, other factors are equally important. Ultimately, you will be happy and fulfilled only if truck dispatching provides you with the challenges and working conditions that make you want to get up and go to work each day.

As with any industry, the best way to decide is to weigh the pros of the business against the cons. And please note that this is from my experience.

So let's start with the advantages:

1. **No formal education or degree is required.**

This is one part about dispatching I love so much. You do not have to hold a bachelor's degree, master's degree, or even associate's degree to start or succeed in the trucking business. In fact, in some cases, you do not even have to have a high school diploma. The truck dispatching business is all about what you put into it and what you make of it, and you can quickly master the game just by doing all I tell you to do in this guide. There is no need to spend hundreds of thousands of dollars obtaining a degree. And once you are ready to start, you can do that from the comfort of your home.

2. Its capital is low

You can start the freight dispatching business with as low as $250 to $550. But then it can cost a few hundred dollars to purchase ancillary materials like printers, scanners, and multiple monitors at the later stages of the business. And when you compare the cost of starting a freight dispatching business to other businesses, you will discover it's a cheaper option.

3. It offers networking opportunities

Another aspect of this business I love to talk about is the networking part. I love meeting new people, talking, and networking with them. I find pleasure in learning and love sharing what I know. So meeting new people will always be an advantage for me because I meet new people from across the U.S. every day and get to network and share information.

Next, let's look at the disadvantages of the trucking business:

1. You have to take calls 24/7

A dispatcher's life is a fast-paced affair of ringing phones and constantly changing load boards. It was tough when I started, as I had to learn to adjust to the 24/7 phone calls and text messages. For instance, let's say you ask a driver to deliver a load to a customer, but then the truck breaks down. The driver will call you because they depend on you to help him find and send a technician to the location where the breakdown occurred.

Or maybe the driver needs a tow truck; in that case, you will have to assist with that. Meanwhile, you will have to contact the owner-operator or carrier to update them about the load's status. Again, I had to adjust to the 24/7 routine because I was used to working a nine-to-five. So once you can adapt to the 24/7 life, nothing will stop you.

2. Finding carriers or owner-operators can be stressful

Even though I had this trouble when I started my dispatching business, you should not experience it since I will show you how to deal with it. Follow all the steps we will cover in the later part of this guide, such as leveraging social media platforms to network with dispatchers, owner-operators, and carriers. You will have an abundance of customers.

Like every business, freight dispatching has its share of stress, but with all that you will learn in this guide, you will learn to manage it. Since trucking is a service industry, it is also demanding, with substantial pressure in most positions. In this day and age, customers demand fast, dependable service, and only people who thrive on pressure and challenges can enjoy many of the industry's opportunities. As a dispatcher, you have to deal with many brokers, shippers, and drivers, and there are many moving factors you have to care about constantly. So the key is to stay organized, think quickly, and learn to adapt to situations.

You should also carefully consider your personality type. Trucking is a people business, and in almost every case, the job calls for a person with an outgoing personality who enjoys interacting and working with other people.

You need to be a team player, as you'll find that trucking companies are only as good as their weakest workers. Every sector in the trucking industry is crucial to the success of the dispatching business. For example, the best drivers in the world won't be working very long if the sales force doesn't secure enough freight to keep them busy. Likewise, an outstanding sales force can only be successful if the operations department provides the quality of service that the customer wants and needs. Likewise, minor operations efforts can move the freight only if the maintenance department keeps the equipment in good operating condition. And the best-maintained equipment will work efficiently only when safety and insurance do their part to establish a good safety record so insurance can be obtained to cover that equipment. Those are just a few examples of the importance of teamwork in the trucking industry.

Getting Started with Freight Dispatching

Today's trucking industry faces a severe shortage of qualified dispatchers. Consequently, wages and benefits are improving, and significant progress has been made to bring improved technology and higher safety standards to the industry. However, the industry needs qualified, safety-conscious professionals committed to the on-time, safe delivery of goods.

If you have what it takes—if you want to contribute to an industry with boundless opportunities—then prepare to work hard and be patient. Also, know your onions and build loyal relationships with brokers and carriers.

The good news is that the truck dispatch business already has a working system. That means you don't have to think of how to create money from scratch; there is already a good flow of money. As a result, several opportunities abound for you as a dispatcher in the trucking industry.

For instance, you can help the carriers find drivers, find loads, work with brokers, build relationships, and maintain or grow their business. Brokers often need help working with carriers, finding excellent and loyal carriers, and wanting to grow their manufacturer and customer base. Suppliers or manufacturers usually face problems because they are busy making products and services. Thus, they have logistics problems for the products they want to ship, which is why they look for reliable brokers with a good carrier base to handle their loads. As you can see, the opportunities are limitless.

Nevertheless, you shouldn't come into the business for the sole purpose of making money. 95% of independent dispatchers fail because they focus solely on money (solving their own problems) instead of their customers' problems. If you focus solely on your needs, you may earn some money. But money will chase your pants down if you focus on solving problems.

Key Takeaway

1. The trucking industry is not just about moving freight—it's about being a part of an increasingly sophisticated logistics system that will keep the nation's economy competitive.

2. A factoring company is a third-party financing company that helps owner-operators and carriers avoid lengthy payment delays on invoices.

3. Freight dispatchers work hard behind the scenes on a mix of support, operations, and customer service tasks to guarantee a particular consignment reaches its

destination at the appointed time.

4. As a dispatcher, your role is to keep portfolios of your carrier's lane preferences, desired freight rates, and equipment specifications.

5. Dispatchers with just one truck typically charge 3–8% of their fee. Using semi-trucks, for example, you can make around $240 to $640 per week and $960 to $2,560 per month.

6. Trucking is a people business, and in almost every case, the job calls for a person with an outgoing personality who enjoys interacting and working with other people.

CHAPTER 2

How to Start Your Dispatching Business Immediately

"Don't worry about failure; you only have to be right once."

— Drew Houston

By now, you must have seen how the trucking industry is one of the major booming sectors of the U.S. economy. Thousands of trucks, trains, ships, and cargo aircraft travel across the nation every day to deliver supplies. For instance, in the United States, trucks alone transport over 71% of the country's freight in terms of weight. And people registered around 33.8 million trucks for commercial use in 2016 alone.

Commercial truck drivers would be lost without dispatchers, which shows how critical the dispatcher's role is in the transportation industry. Luckily, starting a dispatching business is no rocket science, and you can even start one from the comfort of your home.

If you are ready to start your dispatching business immediately, start by knowing which work mode option is right for you, the business setup process, legal requirements, and the technical terms and industry jargon. That way, you will be on the path to becoming a professional independent truck dispatcher. Fortunately, that is what we will study throughout this entire chapter.

Essential Things You Need to Know

As an independent dispatcher, you can start the dispatch business as a side hustle without even owning a single truck; you can also work from home to cut costs and have more flexibility. As you have already learned, your responsibility as a freight dispatcher is to give truck drivers all the necessary information for picking up and delivering loads. Then, you can decide to either assign trucks and workers to customers or locate individual loads to match them with trucks with enough space.

As an independent truck dispatcher, you are also responsible for handling all the billing and paperwork for your clients. Therefore, you must have the appropriate computer skills, a reliable internet connection, and practical communication abilities. You might also offer other services like checking suppliers' or brokers' creditworthiness, negotiating load rates, and offering round-the-clock assistance. These activities require specific equipment, which we will cover in detail here and in subsequent sections.

Working Remotely as a Truck Dispatcher

You can decide to work as an independent contractor or a full-time employee in a carrier company where you have the option to work remotely. Receiving requests for trucks, organizing drivers, and managing load delivery are all part of your job as a remote truck dispatcher. You must also serve as a point of contact for motorists who are already on the road and require more information.

If you want to work remotely as a freight dispatcher, you must have excellent communication, computer, and organizational skills to manage schedules and route planning. You must also have a good phone, computer, internet connection, and scanner in your home to book loads from anywhere and complete other tasks. Working remotely as a truck dispatcher is ideal if you seek the flexibility of a work-from-home job.

Can You Work as a Dispatcher Part-Time?

The short answer is yes; you can work as a dispatcher part-time. But the truth is that running a part-time dispatch business is complicated. Like most careers, you cannot dedicate only half of yourself to the job. You must be ready to dedicate more time to work as a dispatcher. In taking the brave step to work in the trucking industry, you must be willing to make a significant sacrifice. Here is an illustration:

Let's say you have one truck and managed to get one client. You wake up around 8 a.m. and log into your load board to search for details on some loads. Fortunately, you may find something before 8:30 a.m., complete all the paperwork, and get a driver to dispatch the load by 9 a.m. At this point, you may say you are done for the day.

However, around 1 p.m., your client (carrier) may call to tell you the driver has arrived, but that particular load is not ready for transport, so the driver would have to wait two days to get the load. And so, your client may ask you to find a new load for the truck. But to do this, you must return to your load board to repeat the process and book another load for the driver.

Now, you could quickly spare some time to do the task if you work remotely. But if you have another job as a receptionist in an organization, it would be challenging to juggle your responsibilities in both jobs. Eventually, your client will be dissatisfied, and you may get fired sooner or later.

Looking at this illustration, you will agree that you must be accessible to your clients at least during working hours to work as a dispatcher part-time. However, other factors you want to consider are that most of the job requires you to assist carriers with the load booking process, and those load postings are limited outside regular hours. And even though most loads are posted on load boards between 8 a.m. and 5 p.m., many carriers prefer to get the job done in the morning.

How Much Does It Cost to Start as an Independent Truck Dispatcher?

The capital for a truck dispatching business ranges from $1,000 to $2,500, which is less than that of many other businesses. That's because you may already have the necessary tools to successfully run your trucking business from home.

The cost of setting up a truck dispatching business can be classified into two categories: one-time fees and recurring fees.

One-time fees include payment for things like a computer, printer, phone, office supplies, etc., while recurring costs include phone bills, Fax and emails, load board subscriptions, payment for dispatching software, and bookkeeping.

As we proceed, you will learn more about the exact equipment and tools you need to operate your dispatching business successfully.

What Exactly Do You Need?

As with most other jobs, job sites are the best place to find truck dispatcher opportunities. But, then again, you could always approach a carrier and express your interest in working as a truck dispatcher.

While requirements can vary, at the very least, many employers will require a high school certificate or GED and previous customer service experience. In addition, you might inquire if they will train or provide you with entry-level positions.

Many people would much rather work as an employee for one company than as an independent truck dispatcher. However, if you see working as a truck dispatcher as a business opportunity, things can get even more fascinating. And this right here is our focus for this comprehensive guide.

Learning the necessary information is the first step in

becoming an independent truck dispatcher, and that is precisely what you are doing now. You can proceed to the next stage once you understand truck dispatching and how to set up the business.

I have taken the time to break down the process of starting a truck dispatching company below, so take your time to study through it.

1. **Business Setup**

In every state, the law states that if you charge a service fee, you must obtain a license from the state or create a legal business entity. Therefore, you must register your business, apply for a license, and make it compliant to operate your truck dispatching business legally. But I recommend you check with your state to determine whether you need a license to run your dispatching business or just registering it will do.

You must file for a business entity before filing taxes for the current year. So, for example, if the last date for filing is April 15, 2023, but you file on January 16, 2023, without having an LLC, that would be illegal. So therefore, you must get a business entity set up right away.

- **Choose a business name:** Selecting a name for your firm and registering it formally are the first steps in becoming an independent truck dispatcher. Being concise and direct is crucial when naming your company. Use keywords like dispatch, dispatching, freight dispatch, truck dispatch, etc., so people can easily find you. You can use GoDaddy to check if your preferred name is available.

- **Determine your structure:** After deciding on a name, apply for your Employer Identification Number (EIN) with the IRS, DUN, and Bradstreet Number—all of which are free. Afterward, you may decide which business structure to use. It could be a sole proprietorship, Limited Liability Company (LLC), corporation, or partnership structure. While you can file yearly with S-Corp, I recommend you apply for an LLC structure where you will have to file quarterly or annually to avoid penalties.

- **File LLC Formation Documents with your state:** Forms known as LLC Formation Documents must be submitted to your state to create your LLC. Every state has specific forms you will need to use to create your LLC, and the timeline varies from one day to one month.

The business setup cost varies by state, ranging from $250 to $550. Once you have registered your business, you can set up a business bank account.

You should also make drafts of some of the contracts that are crucial to the operation of your dispatching business. This covers the dispatcher-carrier contract, which guarantees the carrier's insurance will protect you against liability if something goes wrong with the freight, and you're not at fault. In addition, you can start working for your partners more quickly if you have drafts of these documents prepared.

2. Compliance—Legalities of Dispatching Business

I have seen some people argue that being a work-from-home dispatcher is illegal since dispatchers don't get their authority or sign a surety bond like brokers. But this is false.

You don't need a bond to be a dispatcher. In fact, you couldn't even apply for a dispatcher bond if you wanted. However, if we examine the situation critically, we will see that a dispatcher owns a dispatching company, and a trucking company hires them as a company to book loads for them in exchange for a service fee. As a truck dispatcher, you use trucking companies' MC numbers whenever you call a broker to book loads for them.

So just like a single person can work for multiple companies, you could also work for multiple trucking companies and receive multiple w-2s every year. And as long as you take care of your tax liabilities, the IRS doesn't care how many jobs you have. But that doesn't mean you should manage too many jobs; instead, manage only what you can handle.

Also, the FMCSA website, where dispatchers are called bona-fide agents, says the only requirement to operate within the law is to always obtain a dispatcher carrier agreement before booking a load. It also says that a dispatcher can sign this agreement for more than one owner-operator. You can refer to the FMCSA site at https://www.ecfr.gov/current/title-49/subtitle-B/chapter-III/subchapter-B/part-371 for further information.

3. Address and Phone

You want a business phone or a Google number so that carriers do not call your private line. However, if you prefer using your private line when starting, you are free to. But I recommend setting up a professional voicemail and answering all calls in case the caller is your carrier, broker, or receiver. Also, while you don't have to do it right away, you could get a virtual address if you want to add your business on Google and your business cards.

4. Home Office Setup

Prepare your workplace for the job. You will need basic computer knowledge and a working computer with a good internet connection and a printer, at the very least. Invest in a good phone system so you can efficiently communicate with partners, suppliers, and drivers. Now, let's look at everything you'll need in more depth.

- **Headphones:** A decent-quality headset with a microphone. This is essential for clear communication.
- **Cell phone:** A simple phone would be sufficient when you are starting. But later, you can switch to voice-over IP, where you can have a phone number and phone service through your internet that you can even use when you are abroad.
- **Computer:** You need a computer with at least 1 TB of space because you need to store many documents in organized folders that are adequately categorized. The computer should have the latest processor of at least Core i5 and a minimum of 16 GB RAM because you will be working with multiple open windows. For instance, you may have many tabs open and be doing your invoicing with calculators. I promise you, the last thing you want is your computer freezing when you are on the phone with your carrier, looking for some freight.
- **Tablet or laptop:** I would not recommend a tablet, but if you are on the go, you may use one. Just make sure the tablet has a good processor, RAM, and at least 1 TB of space.
- **Multiple monitors:** You may start with one monitor, but

after a while, it is wise to add multiple monitors instead of opening loads of tabs. Fortunately, monitors are relatively inexpensive, especially for devices that can significantly improve your productivity.

- **Scanner and printer:** You will be responsible for completing all carrier packets that will be sent to you in paper form via email; as a result, you will have to print and fill them out and then scan and send them back to the broker. So you will need a scanner and a printer.

  You don't need a color printer, as a black-and-white printer will usually do. You can also fill out the form digitally, which is my favorite option because you can do it from your computer or smartphone. Some brokers now even offer digital forms to fill carrier packets. Again, you don't need to send it back; once you fill it and hit the finish button, it automatically goes to the broker.

- **Fax machine:** Instead of buying a fax machine, you use electronic fax services, which allow users to create, sign, and send faxes from their email to anyone anywhere. That way, you don't have to print or scan documents when you need to fax them while dispatching.

- **Office desk/corner desk:** You need a comfortable desk with plenty of space. Instead of putting a lot of sticky notes and décor, it is best to keep the setup minimal and organized so that you can focus on your job. Avoid clutter and keep only the essential things on the desk.

- **Dispatching software:** The use of dispatch software is one of the most crucial resources in any dispatching process. Higher operational efficiencies brought about by good dispatch software might result in cost savings. Researching and investing in such software should not be rushed because dispatching software solutions often require significant financial commitment.

- I recommend getting a decent transportation management system (TMS) like Trucking Office. You can also search for "Trucking Office training" on YouTube to watch tutorial videos. **I have included a detailed guide containing all our recommendations for dispatcher equipment and services. You can find it under Free Bonus #12. So go ahead and check it out.**

Next, you will need all information about your carrier, including their name, MC and DOT numbers from their carrier profile, and their payment information for mailing payments or bank account if they're going to be paid by direct deposit. Also, you will always need a copy of their carrier authority, certificate of insurance (COI), Notice of Assignment (NOA), and w-9. I usually have a separate file for all carriers, both electronically and in paper form, so I can go right to their file when I have to pull a load for a particular carrier. This means that you must be able to organize your files accordingly.

5. Marketing Plan

Please take the necessary actions to launch your truck dispatching company now that you know how to do it. The next stage is to develop a marketing strategy to advertise your services after you have finished the registration process. You want to establish relationships with trucking companies both domestically and internationally. You also want to join forums and chat boards for your industry, participate in their discussions and promote your company. Below are some tips to help you advertise your truck-dispatching business:

- **Have a website:** Building a website is necessary for developing a strong online presence and marketing plan. Choose a short, simple-to-remember domain name for your website that incorporates your company's name. On websites like GoDaddy, you can check your domain's name availability and also register it. You could also create a logo for your business. I use Fiverr to handle these tasks, so do check out the platform. Vistaprint is another platform that works just as well.

- **Leverage popular social media platforms:** You should create accounts across various social media channels such as Facebook, Instagram, TikTok, and any other popular ones you are comfortable using.

- **Network:** While load boards are a terrific resource for carriers to find loads, building relationships is the key to success in the trucking industry. Not only do you want to begin looking for carriers as soon as possible, but you also want to establish relationships with brokers, owner-operators, shippers, and other dispatchers.

Spend some time establishing connections within the trucking industry. Be intentional with your marketing strategy, pay for sponsored ads, and post articles and helpful information regarding trucking online. You should also consider designing business cards and flyers to share with people and promote your business.

Join forces with governmental institutions, manufacturers, and regional groups that can help publicize your company.

The more you advertise your business, the greater its chances of success. We will cover the marketing aspect in greater detail in Chapter 6, so do hang on.

6. Load Boards

Load boards are online marketplaces that link carriers looking for freight to carry with shippers; they also link brokers with the loads they wish to transfer. These freight exchanges are valuable resources that keep cargo moving and save time for all parties involved.

As a dispatcher, you can find spot rates, lane density, and other helpful industry statistics and data on load boards. Load boards may be free or paid, but we will go explore how load boards work in Chapter 4.

Technical Terms and Industry Jargon

If you want to adapt to the trucking industry, you need to understand its lingo. As a beginner, you are in for a shock.

When I joined the freight dispatching industry, I had no idea what many of the terms below meant. The first time I heard the term "123Loadboard," I thought it was a name tag for a kind of load. It took me a while until I discovered that 123Loadboard is one of the major load board companies out there. It was really embarrassing, you know?

So as a dispatcher, you must learn these technical terms to avoid getting thrown off balance once you meet someone who mentions any of them to you. I have arranged them into categories to help you understand, remember, and refer to them quickly and whenever you want.

1. General Terms

- **Dispatch:** Its definition is "to send off." According to a dispatcher agreement, a dispatcher "sends off" or locates cargo for their carrier.

- **Dispatching:** This refers to how truck dispatchers organize and manage truck drivers' schedules to pick up loads and deliver them on time.

- **Dispatch agreement:** A dispatch agreement is a written agreement between a dispatcher and a carrier, owner-operator, or truck driver that specifies the dispatcher's tasks on the carrier's behalf and the conditions of those tasks.

- **Carrier profile:** The dispatching agreement must be completed and returned with a carrier profile, which is filled by the carrier. The carrier profile is a document that informs the dispatcher of the carrier's requirements for payment, the routes they would like to travel, their weight capacity, and other information. When a dispatcher tailors their load search to the carrier's profile like this, they will find loads faster and more efficiently.

- **Transport:** This means moving loads from one location to another.

2. **Carrier Searches**

- **Carrier:** A trucking company or self-employed individual in the freight transportation industry.

- **Cold calling:** The practice of calling carriers over the phone to offer them your dispatching services.

- **International Fuel Tax Association (IFTA):** The organization that ensures equitable diesel/gasoline taxes.

- **HOS (hours of service):** The number of hours the Department of Transportation (DOT) allows drivers to use their trucks daily.

- **PO (Power Only):** Indicates a truck used to move loaded or empty trucks or continue a load if the original truck is disabled.

- **Team (drivers):** Two drivers working as a team enable the truck to go more miles in a day.

- **Truck:** A freight vehicle placed on a chassis or with undercarriage wheels used for highway hauling.

3. **Load Boards**

- **123Loadboard:** One of the biggest load boards online.

- **Assets:** are the trucks or equipment that a trucking firm or owner-operator possesses.

- **Backhaul:** A backhaul is a load a carrier gets after delivering their original load, which they haul back to their home or the location of their next load.

- **Bobtail (bobtailing):** A driver who operates the truck's power unit without also coupling (or connecting) the truck to the Power Only.

- **Commodity:** The class of items or products being pulled, transported, or shipped is referred to as a commodity.

- **DAT:** Acronym for "Dial-a-Truck," one of the most essential load boards for locating freight.

- **Deadhead miles:** The total miles a truck driver drives with an empty truck, either when it returns to its base or to go pick up a load at a new location.

- **DH-O:** Deadhead origin. DH-O is the number of miles a truck driver has to drive "empty" from their *original* location to where they would pick up a load.

- **DH-D:** Deadhead destination. This is the number of miles a truck driver has to drive "empty" from the drop-off location of the load to their next *destination*.

- **DT:** Date and time.

- **Drops:** Describes where or to who a load is being dispatched.

- **Internet Truck Stop:** Another popular load board, with monthly subscription fees starting from $35.

- **Lane:** When you pick up from one location (the shipper) and then deliver to another (the receiver), point A to point B transportation is called a lane (or a line haul).

- **Load:** A load is a cargo carried by truck.

- **Load boards:** Load boards connect shippers, brokers, and carriers. The freight dispatcher goes to the load boards to find available loads for their client.

- **Loaded miles:** The distance traveled by freight from when it was loaded until a carrier delivered it.

- **MacroPoint:** Tracking software

- **P&D:** Pickup and delivery

- **Picks:** Indicates the location or kind of shipper(s) from which a load is being picked up or shipped out.

- **Rate:** The cost of having a carrier transport the commodity or freight.

- **Rate per mile (RPM):** Total load rate divided by total trip miles.

- **Route:** The path taken by a shipment.

- **TL:** Truckload—that is, the full-weight capacity of an equipment type.

- **Trucker Path:** another popular load board.

- **TMS:** Acronym for "transportation management system," which is a content management system (CMS) or customer relationship management (CRM) system for organizing and keeping track of shippers, brokers, carriers, clients, customers, and assets. An example of a TMS system is AscendTMS.

- **LTL/Partial:** "Less than truckload." Basically, it's part of the full-weight capacity of any equipment type.

4. **Dialogue with Brokers or Shippers**

- **Accessorial pay:** The money a carrier receives for rendering services besides the standard pickup and delivery services.

- **Authority:** In order to move freight inside the United States, the broker and the carrier must both produce documents proving that the FMCSA has permitted them.

- **Book a Load:** Once the carrier has been "set up" under the brokerage, approved through compliance, and signed a "load tender" or "rate confirmation," a load can be booked by getting the carrier and broker to agree to take it at an acceptable rate.

- **Broker:** The freight broker is the middleman between the carrier and the shipper.
- **CPM (cents per mile):** CPM is the ratio of the cost of a load to the number of miles it traveled.
- **COI (certificate of insurance):** Most insurance policies include at least $100,000 in cargo coverage and $1,000,000 in liability coverage.
- **Carrier packet:** A form brokers ask carriers to fill out to set them up under their brokerage.
- **Certificate holder:** A third party interested in the insured's capacity to provide adequate coverage for the cargo. While the carrier is under the load, brokers will typically request inclusion in the policy.
- **Claim:** Compensation made to a carrier by a shipper or consignee for an overcharge, loss, or damage to loads being transported.
- **Driver assist:** This fee is added to a shipment if the driver is tasked with loading or unloading the shipment from their truck.
- **DOT number:** A Department of Transportation identification number. Companies that drive commercial vehicles to transport people or goods must register with the FMCSA and obtain a USDOT number.
- **ETA:** This means "estimated time arrival," which is the amount of time a carrier expects a load to take before getting to the shipper or receiver.

- **Equipment Type:** A carrier drives this kind of truck. The three most common ones are a 48'/53' flatbed, a 53' reefer, and a 53' dry van. Hotshots are 40' trucks attached to 3500 double trucks, and 26' straight box trucks are other, less common equipment kinds.

- **FMCSA:** FMCSA stands for Federal Motor Carriers Safety Administration, a department of transportation agency in the United States that oversees the trucking sector.

- **Fuel surcharge or FSC:** Extra compensation a carrier gets when fuel prices increase.

- **Load PO# or Pickup Number:** This number identifies the load picked up from the shipper and delivered to the receiver.

- **Load availability:** When a carrier or dispatcher inquires about the availability of an advertised load from a broker or shipper, the term "load availability" is used.

- **Load/unload pay:** If the carrier must "touch" the freight during loading and unloading, they will be charged a load/unload pay fee.

- **Lumper:** A person hired by the carrier, driver, or owner-operator to load or unload their truck at the shipper or receiver, respectively.

- **MC#:** The FMCSA issues a motor carrier number to a business (broker) or independent contractor (carrier) to permit freight transfer.

- **NOA (notice of assignment):** An NOA is a document that a factoring company requests from a carrier about its broker to enable them to run a credit check to see if the broker has a good credit standing.

- **Rate confirmation (rate con):** Also known as load tender, this is the final document that the carrier or dispatcher receives from the broker, signs, and returns to complete the paperwork and book the load.

- **Shipper:** The person or company who owns or supplies the load/cargo; they are also known as consignors.

- **TONU:** TONU stands for "Truck Ordered, Not Used" and is essentially a cancellation payment made directly to a truck driver when a load is abruptly canceled.

- **Tarp pay:** The fee the carrier charges for the time-consuming task of tarping a load.

- **W-9:** Businesses use the personal information from Form W-9 to complete Form 1099-MISC, which is the report of independent contractors' payments to the IRS.

5. **Invoicing and Payments**

- **Bill of lading (BOL.):** The carrier receives this documentation at the pickup location to confirm that the load has been accepted and inspected and that the carrier is responsible for ensuring its safe delivery.

- Carrier invoice: This document consists of the BOL and the POD that the carrier submits to the broker or their factoring firm for payment.

- **Dispatcher invoice:** When a carrier has gotten empty and delivered the load for which they were initially dispatched, the dispatcher sends the carrier an invoice, which is known as a dispatcher invoice.

- **POD (proof of delivery):** It is submitted by the carrier as a requirement for payment.

6. **Equipment Types**

    - **Air ride suspension:** Instead of using steel springs to support the weight, air ride suspensions use air-filled rubber bags.

    - **Blocking or bracing (dunnage):** These are different sizes of timber used in or on the truck as blocking to make the cargo easier to unload.

    - **Dry van:** The most popular vans (box trucks) on the road today are 48 feet long by 96 inches wide, 48 feet long by 102 inches wide, 53 feet long by 96 inches wide, and 53 feet long by 102 inches wide. The rear doors on these trucks can swing open or roll up.

    - **Flatbed:** A truck transporting heavy objects like coiled steel, lumber, machinery, etc. It has no sides or a top.

    - **E-tracks (vertical vs. horizontal):** These are installed on the walls of a truck; they give you anchor points for tie-downs and allow you to secure equipment.

    - **Load bars:** Load bars are used to secure cargo for transport, so they don't impact one another and get damaged.

    - **Lowboy:** A lowboy trailer is a unique type of trailer with two drops in deck height for transporting heavy loads.

    - **RGN (Removable Gooseneck):** It's usually a flatbed truck connected by a gooseneck to the truck.

    - **Reefer:** A refrigerated truck with a Temperature Control Unit (TCU) connected to a semi-truck used for transporting perishables and other temperature-sensitive items.

- **Step deck:** An elevated deck at the front of the truck's flatbed.
- **Straps:** Used to secure a weight, these typically 4" wide straps are composed of high tensile cloth.
- **Stretch truck:** The term "stretch truck" refers to a flatbed truck having movable rails that may be extended to carry exceptionally long cargo.
- **Tarp:** A type of weather-proof material used for covering exposed loads in flatbed trucks.

Key Takeaway

1. As an independent truck dispatcher, you are also responsible for handling all the billing and paperwork for your clients.
2. A truck dispatcher must have the appropriate computer skills, a reliable internet connection, and practical communication abilities.
3. You must register your business, apply for a license, and make it compliant to operate your truck dispatching business legally.
4. Invest in a good phone system so you can efficiently communicate with partners, suppliers, and drivers.
5. After registering your business, develop a marketing strategy to foster relationships with trucking companies both domestically and internationally.

CHAPTER 3

GETTING YOUR FIRST CARRIER

"Always deliver more than expected."

— Larry Page

ONCE YOU HAVE understood the basics of truck dispatching, decided it's the right business opportunity for you, and worked towards setting up your dispatching business, what's next?

Of course, finding your first carrier is the next task to cross out on your to-do list.

Now, when it comes to finding carriers to work with, there are certain factors you want to pay attention to. For instance, you want to ensure you use the right equipment, understand how to approach the carrier, have the necessary documents, and know several other important details. So let's dive right into it!

Common Equipment Types

When starting your freight dispatch business, one challenge you may face is choosing from various trucking equipment types. I faced this issue when I first entered the trucking industry. For instance, each type of trailer has different considerations, and I couldn't just tell the right one to use in a particular situation.

Also, brokers will usually request specific equipment types, and you want to ensure you send the right tools. Most times, many dispatchers ignore details or aren't sure of what equipment is requested, so they send their drivers with the wrong equipment. What they need to realize is they are losing time.

Your driver may reach their destination only to realize that you gave them the wrong equipment and so can't load the truck, which could upset them. For example, it could be they don't have tarps, aren't hazmat carriers, or don't have a removable gooseneck.

You want to pay detailed attention to the types of trucking equipment you'll be working with and when to use them. Luckily, I have already compiled a list for you, so keep reading to learn more about each equipment type and decide which one to use for your trucking business.

1. **Reefer Trucks**

A reefer is a refrigerated truck typically used for transporting chilled or frozen equipment that requires a temperature-controlled environment. Your carrier will ask for this type of trailer whenever they need a load transported from the pickup point to the drop-off point at a specified temperature.

I love working with reefers because it's such an exciting experience, especially during the seasons I have to handle shipments of loads like cherries or watermelons. Although working with reefers can be challenging as it involves more responsibilities from you as the dispatcher and your driver, it's easier when you learn how it works.

You want to have a Reefer Breakdown Policy if a mechanical breakdown occurs. But, you know, sometimes, there can be human errors, such as your driver not using the right setting. For example, let's say you tell your driver you want the temperature set at 24°C, but instead, he puts it at 34°C, and on reaching the drop-off point, the load is rejected. In that case, your Reefer Breakdown Policy won't cover such a mistake since it's a human error and not a mechanical fault.

When working with reefers, you also want to ensure their units are well maintained and all other essential factors are well in place. These include the following:

- **Reefer air ride:** This helps with transporting loads with safety and comfort. For example, let's say you are asked to transport fragile items, like crates of eggs or cartons of fish; you don't want your driver delivering them cracked or messed up, right? So while you want to take the extra step to strap such items securely to the reefers, check the reefer air ride to ensure it works.

- **Reefer double:** This one is easy to understand as it's a reefer van with two or double refrigerated compartments. Always ensure that your driver has the endorsement on their commercial driver's license (CDL) to operate a reefer double or triple.

- **Reefer hazmat (RZ):** This reefer type is like any other but hauls hazardous materials. For this reefer, you want to pay good attention to the temperature requirement. Let's say you're transporting a medical item with the temperature requirement set in Celsius but have your RZ set in Fahrenheit, you need to tell the driver to do the conversion, or you can also do it yourself. This will help prevent cargo claims and make you a professional dispatcher.

- **Reefer intermodal:** Reefer intermodal is the word used to describe the transportation of refrigerated containers and trailers through a combination of long-haul train, air, water, and first- and last-mile trucking. Even though there are many good reasons to transport temperature-controlled cargo by truck, those who don't think about reefer intermodal are missing out on major capacity opportunities by not using the same refrigerated trailers that trucks and refrigerated intermodal contain.

- **Reefer logistics:** Temperature-sensitive cargo such as food, electronics, chemicals, or pharmaceutical products must be sent following strict specifications. But what happens when you transport different loads with different temperature requirements, such as +35°C and -20°C? This is where reefer logistics come in. To avoid the load getting rejected, you want to make sure you use the right equipment type and not just try to combine stuff. What you need to do is get a reefer trailer with bulkheads or try to install them on your reefer trucks. But try not to do it yourself.

- **Reefer with pallet exchange (RP):** Sometimes, your shipment may require pallet exchange. A pallet is used to support a load steadily when being raised by a forklift, pallet jack, upright crane, and so on. As a professional, you can buy palettes if you work with carriers that don't offer pallet exchange; they usually cost from $6 to $10. You can also negotiate for them to reimburse you. And they can, as long as you still have the purchase receipt.

- **Reefer with a team:** Some carriers would prefer to have a reefer with a team to increase productivity. This means you'll need two or more people driving together to deliver the load faster.

2. **Dry Van Trailers**

A dry van is an enclosed trailer for carrying freight that cannot be exposed to external elements. Drivers may load cargo onto dry van trailers using a loading dock behind the truck. Dry vans, which can be size 53' or 48', are commonly used for transporting goods such as clothing, furniture, machinery, electronics, non-perishables, and other household items.

When working with dry van trailers, you want to ensure their units are well maintained and all other essential factors are in place. These include the following:

- **Van air ride:** Just like the reefer air ride, the van air ride has something to do with the suspension of that trailer so that the load can be transported safely.

- **Van Conestoga:** Van Conestoga features a retractable tarping system spanning the length of its decks. This van offers the ability to secure cargo ranging from many groups of palletized products to large equipment, which also makes loading and unloading incredibly simple. Essentially, Van Conestoga is designed to protect big and specialized loads from the outdoors without damaging delicate equipment, paint, coatings, or other aspects of your cargo that can be damaged if a tarp is placed over the load.

- **Van double:** Again, this is similar to a reefer double or triple. So you need to ensure your driver has the endorsement on his CDL.

- **Van hazmat:** Similar to the RZ, a van hazmat is used for transporting unique materials. So you need to ensure your driver uses the correct placards correctly so they won't get any violations when they get stopped.

- **Van hotshot:** We use van hotshot to transport smaller cargo and reach areas where big trucks cannot go. Imagine you are required to transport a load to a busy neighborhood like New York City; you wouldn't want to go with a big truck like van 53'. In this case, a small van works perfectly like the van hotshot.

- **Van insulated (VI):** This type of van protects the load from heat and cold and can be in different sizes, too, such as 48' or 53'.

- **Van intermodal:** Like the reefer intermodal, a van

intermodal is a trailer for transporting air, water, or rail.

- **Van liftgate:** This is a mechanical device permanently mounted on the back of a van. It is designed to make it easier to move loads from a loading dock or the ground to the level of the vehicle bed, or vice versa.

- **Van open top:** It's a van designed for the load to be loaded from the top. We also use this equipment type in the agricultural sector to transport building materials. Although the regular trucking company works with them frequently, you may need to use them when working for somebody in this field.

- **Van roller bed:** This tool has wheels that you can easily position and transport a load from one point to another.

- **Vented van:** Most dry and non-perishable items are shipped using a vented van. Vents are installed at the front and back of the trailer for air circulation and weather protection.

- **Van with the blanket wrap:** Sometimes, you'll need to transport loads like furniture or particular commodities on a van open top. When this happens, you'll need to cover the load with blankets to protect them.

- **Van with the pallet exchange:** This works just like the RP, which we already covered in the previous section.

- **Van with a team:** Your client would sometimes request a van with a team to make the job easier. So you want to have this at the back of your mind.

3. **Flatbed Trucks**

Due to their adaptability and capacity restrictions, flatbed trucks are among the most popular trucking equipment types. Flatbed trucks do not have an enclosed area surrounding the freight like a standard trucking container. As a result, flatbed drivers may transport oversized goods faster than they could with a regular dry van.

The regular flatbeds can be sized 48' or 53' and have a different scale. So when you ask your driver about their truck, you want to make sure you ask the driver for the truck's scale ticket.

Scale tickets are provided as heavyweight or lightweight and give the truck weight when loaded versus when it's empty. We use the scale ticket to determine the net billable weight, which becomes part of the shipment paperwork.

Some common loads you can haul with flatbeds include auto parts, construction equipment, excavators, lumbers, large electrical equipment, long steel bars, etc. Here are some of the things you need to pay attention to when working with flatbeds:

- **Flatbed air ride:** You want to ensure your flatbed has a good air ride—that is, the air suspension that helps protect your loads from getting damaged during haulage. You also don't want to forget your load locks, straps, and e-tracks, which you need to secure your load firmly to the flatbed truck.

- **Flatbed Conestoga:** This combines a Conestoga and flatbed on the same trailer. We use the flatbed Conestoga to transport many of the same open-deck loads as the traditional flatbed.

- **Flatbed double:** We have the regular flatbed and the flatbed double trailer, which are connected by two flatbed trailers. A flatbed double is suitable for shipping various bulk loads and provides easier loading and unloading.

- **Flatbed hazmat:** We use this to haul hazardous materials. This means that your company has to be a hazmat carrier and has higher insurance coverage. And, yes, your driver needs to be hazmat certified on his CDL.

- **Flatbed hotshot:** This is a smaller flatbed used for hauling loads with a lower weight. But you must still abide by the same rules and policies guiding regular flatbeds.

- **Flatbed maxi:** This is a typically flatbed but which carries more weight than the regular flatbeds.

- **Flatbed over dimensional:** You can't have more than a legal size for a flatbed. So here you need to understand the size; you know, the flatbed can be 160ft long, 18 ft high, and 18ft wide and carry a load of around 200,000 pounds. This is why we call it flatbed over-dimensional. So you need to have special permits and know how to negotiate to use this kind of truck. You'll need to pay tolls, understand the rules of moving from state to state, and know what liability you may incur along the line.

- **Flatbed with chains:** Flatbed with chains helps you to haul goods that need to be firmly secured to the truck. Of course, this is a special requirement, and clients pay more for this option and the extra services.

- **Flatbed with side:** We usually use this special equipment in construction. They aren't pretty-looking trailers but are solid and can last several years.

- **Flatbed with tarps:** Here, you want to know if your driver's truck has tarps, the number of tarps they have, and their specific sizes. As a professional dispatcher working with flatbeds, you'll leave a lot of money on the table if you refuse to haul loads that need tarping. This is because working with loads requiring tarping calls for extra work and charges.

- **Flatbed with a team:** Working as a team is very common with flatbeds since you'll be hauling a bigger load. Again, this will cost your client extra money as they must pay for the team services. Sometimes we have a team, and a broker tells me they want a flatbed with a team but want to pay for the solo transit. I tell them it's not possible. They have this cargo and want it delivered within a few days and enjoy excellent service from our team, so why would they refuse to pay? What I do is negotiate with them so we can get duly compensated.

4. **Power-Only Trucks**

We use power-only trucking to transport loads using a semi-truck (a kind of tractor or trailer head) and driver. Power-only trucks are less common than the others because drivers don't use them to haul loads. So when you see a power-only truck in transit, it's either heading to a load or returning from one.

Let's say your driver lives in New York and decides he wants a reefer. But the reefer is in Washington, and he doesn't want to drive empty. In this case, you can get him a power-only truck, and usually, they will give you a trailer for seven to ten days, and you will need to bring it somewhere, like Boston, for instance.

But you can still load the trailer and use it for some time; usually, they'll pay you $150 to $400 for the haulage.

Now, the question is, how do you make money?

It's simple! You make money by putting the load on that trailer. Also, you make money for your driver since they're not driving empty from New York to Washington. And you make money for the company since they bring the trailer from half way across the country for around $400.

But then, this is business, and the last thing someone will do is give you a power-only truck if you don't have a trailer inter-exchange policy. So if you are working with power-only, you need to make sure you have a trailer inter-exchange policy since you'll be hooking with somebody else's equipment. And the power-only has to be protected should you damage it or somebody scratches it.

5. **Other Equipment Trucks**

Now, aside from these four major equipment types, we have covered, there are others you want to pay attention to:

- **Auto Carrier (AC):** This type of trailer or semi-trailer is designed to transport passenger vehicles via truck efficiently.
- **B train:** This road freight transport is larger than a semi-trailer but shorter than a road train. So it's more of like a truck-trailer combination.
- **Step deck:** This is an open flatbed trailer with a step or drops at the front at the gooseneck, allowing a slightly lower deck than a standard flatbed.

- **Step deck Conestoga:** This is simply a step deck with a Conestoga, so it's more special than Conestoga. And, yes, it costs more than the regular Conestoga.

- **Straight/box truck:** A straight truck, sometimes known as a "box truck" or "cube truck," is a commercial vehicle with several axles connected by a single frame from the trailer's front to behind the cab. Straight trucks come in various lengths and are distinguished by their box-like storage that holds the cargo.

- **Stretch trailer (ST):** This is a special type of equipment to hold long cargo and loads of various lengths.

- **Tanker aluminum (TA):** This tanker is for liquids, usually specific to a single type of liquid unless carefully cleaned. You should check your driver's CDL to ensure they have the endorsement to drive a TA.

- **Tanker intermodal:** A tanker transported on a rail car (trailer on a flat car). This can go on wood, rail, air, and water.

- **Tanker steel:** This is a tanker for hauling liquids, usually specific to a single type of liquid unless carefully cleaned. We usually use it to transport oils and all other chemicals.

When using these equipment types, you should understand that the basics of logistics stay the same. The only differences are the truck type, pricing, fees, and the required special permits. Once you familiarize yourself with these things, your dispatching process will become seamless.

Finding Your First Carrier under Five Minutes

Getting new carriers is something most truck dispatchers struggle with. Carriers don't call looking for a new dispatcher, and even when you reach out to a carrier, you're not always guaranteed to land a deal.

Honestly, finding a good carrier takes deliberate effort. Even as an expert in the industry, I still have to be consistently intentional about what I want in a carrier. Now, when it comes to finding carriers to work with, there are specific approaches you want to take.

Here, I reveal my killer strategy for finding your first carrier and load. Trust me—only elite-level dispatchers know these secrets. So let's dig in.

Let's say today you decided to look for loads and carriers that want to go out of New York City. The first thing to do is search for trucks, and I use a load board app like the DAT

Power to do this. The DAT platform makes it easy for you to contact carriers and tell them about your services.

So what you need to do is visit the DAT Power platform and sign up for an account. Under Load board plans, you can choose "Power Select Carrier." Once you log in to your dashboard, use the "Post Trucks" option to search for trucks by entering the requested details such as load origin, load destination, the truck's weight, length, capacity, and your desired search back time.

So let's say you want a truck of 53 ft in length that can carry a load of 45,000 lbs. from New York City to Phoenix, Arizona. You enter the details.

Then enter your desired search back time; in this case, we can decide to check for trucks posted in the past 6 hours.

Of course, you can narrow your search if you want to be more specific.

And once the list of available trucks is shown, you can browse through them to find authorities who have the kind of truck you need.

So let's say you find someone around Scottsdale, and you check further to see their details. The next thing to do is note down the information about the trucks you found.

After that, you need to search for loads.

Remember, you haven't contacted the truck owner yet; you're just trying to see if you can find a load for them.

So you click the search load option and enter the details for the truck you found—that is, its origin, destination, weight, length, and the search back time. Then you browse through the list of loads, reading the descriptions and rate to see which one is good and the best fit.

Once you find one you like, you can call the contact shown to ask for further details about the load. Afterwards, you can put them on hold and ask them to give you some time to contact your driver.

At this point, you should return to the truck details you noted earlier, search for the driver's contact details, and call them. Once the driver answers the call, you introduce yourself to them and ask relevant questions about the truck, confirming every necessary detail.

Once everything checks out, you may tell them you have a load for them and share the details with them. If they ask who you are, you can just tell them you're a truck dispatcher and share your rates with them.

I recommend you offer them the first load for free; you should waive all dispatching fees. And once they develop the initial trust, you can ask for a dispatch fee for later loads.

Honestly, there is no better and faster way to find a carrier than this one. The fascinating aspect of using this method is that you aren't just cold-calling the driver but also offering a solution to their immediate problems—which is they need a load today, and you can do just that.

Recall I told you in Chapter 1 that this is what freight dispatching is all about—solving trucking problems. So that's it!

Once you find loads for several carriers and start making

connections, you will not only kick start your truck dispatching journey, but it'll also become easier and more interesting.

And if you've never heard of the term "load board" and don't understand the illustration I gave adequately, don't worry—it was just to provide you with a birds eye view of the strategy.

In the next chapter, "Finding loads," I've covered all the terms and processes in complete detail and a video tutorial guide. Once you master that section, you can return here to re-read the illustration, and by then, it'll start making sense.

Later, in Chapter 6, I'll show you in great detail how you can leverage various online and offline methods to help you find carriers.

Dispatcher Carrier Agreement to Send Carriers

You will need to email these documents to your carrier, have the carrier sign them, and email them back to you before you can work as their dispatcher. These documents include the following:

1. Dispatcher Service Agreement

A dispatch service agreement is basically a contract between an independent truck dispatcher and the trucking company, carrier, or owner-operator. This agreement acts as proof that the carrier has agreed to your fees and services.

The dispatch service agreement further outlines the relationship between you and your carrier, and it also details you and your carrier's responsibilities. For example, your duty as the dispatcher is to find and book loads for your carrier, while your carrier is responsible for paying you for your services.

Do not make the mistake of working with a carrier without having a dispatch service agreement in place.

Here are three main reasons to sign a service agreement with your carrier:

Authorization: They must permit you to act on their behalf in roles like calling clients, doing the paperwork, and booking a load. If you don't have this permission stated in writing, that technically means you're not authorized to do anything on your carrier's behalf.

Compensation: You want to clearly state how you want to be paid for your services. Maybe it'll be a flat fee or based on a percentage; just make it known. Also, state whether they're to use a credit card or you're to mail them a digital invoice.

Liability: You also want to state that you will be providing an administrative service and that you won't transport any cargo that isn't the responsibility of the trucking company you work for. You may also want to clarify that it's their responsibility to oversee the safety of the operation and that you won't be held responsible if something goes wrong.

Sometimes, you may encounter a carrier that insists they don't need a dispatcher service agreement. I strongly recommend you run away from such clients. Having the agreement in place makes everyone feel comfortable and saves you from unnecessary troubles. **I've provided you with the link to access the Dispatch Service Agreement templates I use for my business at the beginning of this guide, so feel free to check them under Free Bonus #1 later.**

2. **Carrier Profile**

A Carrier Profile is a document containing details from your client on their truck, load preference, and where they would like to haul a load.

The information required to be filled in a Carrier Profile is typically divided into five parts, namely:

Part A—The Carrier Information: This includes the company name, MC number, DOT number, SSN or EIN, SCAC Code, and any available certifications.

Part B—Contact Details: This includes the physical address, mailing address, name of the contact person, email address, office phone number, Fax, and website address.

Part C—Equipment Information: This is where the carrier will state their equipment type, size, weight limit, truck or trailer number, and any other information.

Part D—Dispatch Information: This includes the minimum fee per mile, max pick or pickups, max deliveries, preferred distance runs, preferred zones and routes, insurance company details, and the brokers they're already set up or approved with.

Part E—Carrier Pay: This last section covers the payment information for mailing payments or banking info for direct deposit.

3. Limited Power of Attorney

You'll need limited Power of attorney since you will fax and sign documents on your carrier's behalf.

A limited power of attorney agreement limits the agent's ability to act and make decisions on those activities the principal has permitted them to manage. An attorney is not the same as an attorney at law, so a principal is not required to select an attorney to act as their agent.

If you plan to use the Dispatcher Service Agreement we have provided, then you don't have to worry about obtaining a separate power of attorney since we have added clauses for it inside the same document.

You can copy these agreements and add your logo and information or find other templates online and customize them to fit your needs.

4. Other Documents Needed from the Carrier

Aside from the agreement documents, there are also some documents you will need from your carrier when they agree to hire you as their dispatcher. You need to have these documents on hand if your carrier still needs to be set up with the broker you are trying to book a load with.

If they are not set up with your preferred broker, the broker will email you their carrier packet and request that you send back the following documents:

- **MC Authority:** Carriers register their authority with FMCSA and get the MC Authority document, which shows the MC and DOT number and the date it was granted.

- **Certificate of insurance (COI):** A certificate of insurance (COI) is a non-negotiable document issued by an insurance company confirming that an insurance policy exists. You want to request the COI from your carrier and verify the following:

    » *The COI is authentic:* Just call the insurance company

and provide them with the policy number so they can help you verify the validity of the insurance certificate.

» *It covers the main essentials:* Auto and cargo are the two most essential liability categories for truckers. So you avoid hiring any carrier whose insurance doesn't cover these categories.

» *The policy is current:* you can only guarantee an insurance certificate is valid the day it is issued.

» *Exclusions, limitations, and other coverage types are available:* Insurance certificates only prove that the carrier has insurance; they don't list exclusions or limitations stated in the policy. So if you want to find out if a policy has exclusions or limitations, you can always contact the insurance agent.

- **W-9 Form:** This document is usually required by the broker so they can book a load with the carrier.

- **Notice of assignment (NOA):** NOA is a document issued by factoring companies, and it contains a notice to send all the payments to the factoring company since the carrier is now their "client."

As an independent dispatcher, it is vital to have these documents so that you don't have to ask your carrier for this information when they're busy. This means you should get the information once you establish a relationship with the dispatcher.

What I do is create a folder on my PC with my carrier's name and add all of their documents to their specific folder. It's that easy!

So that's it for now. The next chapter will discuss everything you need to know about finding loads, the booking process, and trip planning. You'll learn more about HOS regulations and the right way to plan a trip for your load haulage. You'll also learn how to call brokers and negotiate rates with them, so they don't exploit you.

Key Takeaway

1. When starting your truck dispatching business, one common challenge is choosing from various trucking equipment types. The most common equipment types are reefers, dry vans, flatbeds, and power-only trucks.

2. Before you can work as a carrier's dispatcher, there are some documents you need to email to them, so they sign and send them back to you. These documents include the dispatcher service agreement and carrier profile.

3. One unique way to win over your first carrier is to offer them the first load for free; that is, you should waive all dispatching fees. And once they develop the initial trust, you can ask for a dispatch fee for later loads.

4. As a dispatcher, you want to check your driver's location, HOS, and availability dates before going to load boards.

Do you like the book so far?

Hey! Sorry to interrupt. I'm just checking in to see if you're enjoying the Freight Dispatcher Training Guide. I can't wait to hear what you think of it!

We would be incredibly grateful if you could leave a picture review on Amazon. If you can't leave a picture review, then even a text review of 1 or 2 sentences would mean a whole lot to us.

To do it, go to your amazon shopping app on your phone, click on that. Once you are inside, click on the top three bars in the left-hand corner and click on "your orders."

From there, you'll be able to see what you've bought. Next, scroll down to the item on which you want to leave a picture review, then click "write a product review."

Once there, select how many stars you want to leave and click the book cover. Then click on the camera icon to add a photo or a video; from there, you can take a picture of the book, click on use photo, and then that photo will be uploaded to your amazon app immediately.

Finally, give it a title and write a little bit of text about what you liked about the book.

Reviews are the best way for small authors – like ours – to get noticed and reach a wider audience. For this reason, your support really does make a difference.

CHAPTER 4

FINDING LOADS

"I don't know the word 'quit.' Either I never did, or I have abolished it."

—*Susan Butcher*

So you've followed the guide in the previous chapter and succeeded in finding your first carrier. Your next goal is to start finding more loads for them immediately!

It doesn't matter if you're new to the truck dispatching business or you've been moving loads for years; finding new loads for your carriers and owner-operators can sometimes be challenging.

Generally, having a steady flow of work—that is, constantly finding loads to move—is the key to succeeding in the truck dispatching business. And you shouldn't underestimate this fact!

Fortunately, we have the technology to help us do this today. And so, our goal for this chapter is to explore several working methods and ways to find loads for your carriers. You will also learn the crucial steps you must take to ensure long-term success.

What Are Load Boards?

Load boards are online matching services that connect shippers to brokers and brokers to carriers or transport owners. These freight exchanges are valuable resources that keep cargo moving and save time for all parties.

The load board acts as a database with every load coming in and out of every state in real-time. And with the increased functionality of internet-based load boards, they have become the most popular method of connecting dispatchers with shipments and maximizing their earnings.

Using load boards to find freight makes the truck dispatching process much faster and more efficient, with enough data always available. This means you can easily access the information you need as a dispatcher to make the right business decisions and access suitable loads.

Fortunately, you've got several options when choosing a load board, including free load boards and subscription-based load boards. But remember that before you can sign up for almost any load board, you'll need to sign up under a carrier with their DOT or MC numbers, though there are some load boards like DAT Power that don't require you to have MC authority. So now, let's quickly check out some popular load boards:

1. **Free Load Boards**

First, we have free load boards, which means they don't require any subscription or payment. The free load board was my go-to choice when I started since I had a tight budget.

So if you're starting and don't have enough funds, free load boards are an excellent way to find some loads and save money. And here are the top free load boards I recommend, as they get updated regularly with fresh loads:

- NextLOAD
- Quick Transport Solutions Inc.
- FreeFreightSearch.com
- Step Deck Carrier
- Freight Terminal
- Werner Logistics and Trucker Tools
- US Logistics
- Trulos.com
- TSH Tennessee Steel Haulers

We also have large companies with load boards, including J. B. Hunt, Total Quality Logistics (TQL), C. H. Robinson, Uber Freight, Pepsi, and Schneider.

You can also book loads directly from the broker's load boards using platforms like XpressTrax.

Since you're just starting, I recommend you sign up and use these free load boards. That way, getting loads for your carriers in no time will be easy.

2. **Subscription-Based Load Boards**

From my experience, subscription-based load boards are the best load boards to use. So if you can afford to invest in them, you shouldn't hesitate, as subscription-based load boards offer many benefits free load boards don't provide.

For instance, instead of just performing a search as you would do with free load boards, subscription-based load boards let you post the trucks you have, and the system will find a load for you. If you can recall, we used the same "Post Truck" feature to find our first carrier in Chapter 3.

All you have to do is fill in all the information about the truck you're finding a load for, such as its origin, destination, weight, and any other special features it may have. Furthermore, subscription-based load boards are the best tools for finding truck loads long-term, especially high-paying loads. And they can cost between $35 and around $350 per month.

Below is a list of the paid load boards I use for my freight business:

- **Trucking Planet:** What I like about this platform is it tells you how often a load runs, whether weekly, daily, monthly or once. So if you are looking for dedicated freight with repeated loads, this information would be helpful. Trucking Planet provides you with the details of direct shippers, including the names, contact emails, and phone numbers of the person in charge. It also tells you the specialization of listed carriers (maybe they're dry van carriers, flatbed carriers, or reefer carriers) and what they do in terms of shipping volume (perhaps it's 10 million, 20 million, or more). And if you are looking for shippers, this platform will tell you which ones are good for dry van shipments, reefer shipments, and so on.

- **Truckstop.com** is another paid option offering basic, advanced, and professional load board features. It also has a mobile app that you can download on your smartphone store to get daily rate information; view live loads in real-time, book loads instantly, save and compare loads later, negotiate with confidence, and factor your load on the go.

- **DAT:** DAT, also known as TruckersEdge, doesn't require a DOT or MC number for you to sign up. This paid load board lets you save your searches to avoid entering the information whenever you look for loads for the same truck. You can even create alerts on your searches to be notified as soon as a perfectly matching load is posted, which should take little time given that hundreds of thousands of new loads are placed daily.

- **Direct Freight Services:** This one is my go-to place for loads. I say so because I'm the first to complain when things get nasty with a load board. But I've found Direct Freight Express really good since I've been using its features. This load board provides tracking updates, straightforward delivery instructions, and good customer service. So you can also check them out.

- **123Loadboard.com:** Another highly regarded load board in the transportation sector is 123Loadboard. Searching for more loads and freight on this platform is quick and straightforward. And you can leverage the Load Planner on 123Loadboard to identify backhauls and cut down on your empty kilometers.

- **Trucker Path:** Trucker Path is a fast-growing load board giving access to over 150,000 loads daily and over two million available loads monthly. You may want to check them out too.

- **Mothership Carrier App:** This app is a good option if you plan on dispatching box trucks. You can download the mobile app and sign up to get matched with local loads near you in real-time.

Although using subscription-based load boards is your best bet, starting with free load boards is okay if you've got a tight budget. Besides, you can always scale up later. Regardless, it would be best to try out as many load boards as possible and weed out the ones you don't like later.

You'll need to get yourself familiar with the common load board terminologies, so you don't miss out on any vital information shown to you across the dashboard. Luckily, we already covered these in Chapter 2, so you should check them out.

Before You Go to Load Boards

As a dispatcher, there are certain things you want to check before going to load boards. And you've to be able to pay attention to detail, especially when working with owner-operators.

On paper, truck dispatching looks pretty simple since it involves moving loads from one point to another. But in reality, it isn't that easy.

As a dispatcher, there are certain things you want to check before going to load boards. And you've to be able to pay attention to detail, especially when working with owner-operators. While you have to work with the owner-operators to plan trips for pickup and delivery, you also need to find drivers and consistently assign them loads based on their HOS and availability.

Here are the few things you must check before you go to load boards:

1. **The Driver's Location**

If you plan to use the dispatch management spreadsheet that we have shared inside the free bonuses, then you should use the truck tracker sub-sheet to track the current location of your drivers. Using this tracker, you'll instantly know which driver needs a new load and their current location.

2. **The Driver's HOS**

Next, you want to calculate the driver's Hours of Service (HOS) using e-logs. This will let you know if your driver has a fresh set of hours to haul the load for that day. If not, you can plan for a new date with them. For instance, if your driver has only 6 hours left, taking a load that requires around 8 hours would be legally impossible. You'll have to choose another date the driver will be available. So knowing your driver's HOS is extremely important. As a dispatcher, this is a significant factor to consider, as there are HOS regulations.

Below are some rules property-carrying drivers must follow, as issued by the Federal Motor Carrier Safety Administration (FMCSA):

- Drivers are only allowed to legally drive a maximum of 11 hours out of their 14 hours workday limit.

- A property-carrying driver may only drive up to the 14 hours workday limit after being off duty for ten straight hours.

- Drivers must take a 30-minute break after driving for 8 hours straight, which they can use to eat or take a bathroom break.

- After working 60 or 70 hours in 7 or 8 straight days, a driver is not permitted to operate a vehicle. After taking 34 or more straight hours off, a driver may restart a 7- or 8-consecutive-day period.

- Drivers may divide their necessary 10-hour off-duty period if one off-duty session is at least two hours long and the other comprises sleeping for at least seven straight hours. Every pair of sleeping berths MUST equal at least 10 hours. Neither session affects the 14-hour driving period when used together.

- In challenging driving cases, drivers may extend the 11-hour maximum driving limit and the 14-hour driving period by 2 hours or less.

You can attach an ELD (also known as an E-log) to your driver's truck to automatically track and record their duty hours. Various apps like Motive (formerly known as KeepTruckin) can also help you track your drivers' HOS.

Finally, you must always check that your new drivers comply with these rules.

3. Driver's Availability

Checking your driver's HOS isn't enough to plan a good trip; you also want to ask them if they are comfortable plying the designated route. You know, they could have specified the routes they don't like or prefer at all while filling carrier profiles. So you can't just book a load to your destination without checking first with your driver.

In addition, you have to put into consideration unforeseen

circumstances. You can't just assume the driver will always be available. They've got their plans, too; they could have an appointment to meet up with, or their truck had just broken down. It could also be that they can't drive beyond specific daily miles for certain reasons.

You need to consider all these factors to enable the driver to deliver the load timely and safely. And while you want to track your driver's HOS and availability, you don't want to make it seem like you're bugging them. I recommend using fleet management software like Motive (formerly KeepTruckin) to track your driver's activity. That way, you let them drive at their own pace while you book loads according to their driving activity. It's as easy as that.

4. **Equipment & Dispatch Details**

When finding loads on any of these load boards I mentioned earlier, you'll need to use the information your carrier provided on their carrier profile form. These include the following:

- Equipment type (Load size, weight, length of the trailer, etc.)
- Minimum Cents Per Mile
- Max weight a trailer can haul
- Max picks and deliveries
- Preferred Routes/ lanes
- Routes/ lanes to avoid

How to Search The Loads

After signing up with your preferred load boards & gathering other necessary details, the next step is mastering how to find cargo for carriers and owner-operators to haul. After all, how else will you keep your dispatch business running during pandemics, freight recessions, capacity shortages, and recoveries? Ultimately, your primary objective as an independent dispatcher is to secure high-paying loads.

As a dispatcher, the best way to boost profitability is to find the highest-paying loads and best freight routes. But not all truckloads pay well, and some routes are less economical than others. So until you find practical solutions to get high-paying truck loads often, your freight dispatch business may not thrive. Fortunately, in this section, I'll walk you through the process of finding loads.

Once you're done logging into a load board dashboard, the next step is to search the load boards for freights. I've prepared a live load board video tutorial where you can see all the steps we'll discuss here with live step-by-step examples. Depending on the load board app you use, you'll have fields to fill in the following details:
- Origin;
- Destination;
- Vehicle Type;
- Availability Dates;
- Deadhead Origin;
- Deadhead Destination;
- Load type—Full load or Partial load; and
- Length, Weight, and Capacity of the equipment you wish to find a load for.

Fill in all these details and hit search to get the search results, and you'll get all the loads available for the details you entered. The next step is to analyze specific factors before considering booking a load. Let's proceed to discuss them all, one by one.

1. Trip Planning

As a dispatcher, the first thing you want to do before booking or considering any loads is to plan the trip properly. And this process is what we call "trip planning."

To understand its importance, let's say, for instance, you have a load in a 53-ft dry van moving out of Nashville, Tennessee, today at 6 p.m., and you contact your driver to pick it up. Then, they finish loading by around 7 p.m. and hit the road at 7:30 p.m.

Meanwhile, the receiver in New York wants the item delivered the next day by 8 a.m. Your job as the dispatcher is to get the information from the broker and work with it. So you check your driver's HOS and factor in the 11-hour driving window.

You also check if that driver did any driving before that 6 p.m. pickup time and see if they can meet up with the 8 a.m. delivery time.

Unfortunately, after considering all these factors, you realize the deadline won't work since the drive time from Nashville to New York is around 14 hours. And when you consider other factors like road closure and weather, meeting the deadline becomes less feasible.

So, what do you do at this point?

Well, that's where trip planning comes in. If you do your homework correctly, you'll easily avoid booking such loads in the first place.

2. Weather conditions

As a dispatcher, I keep my eyes glued on the weather channel because the weather can sometimes be funny. And since the weather does affect your driver, you must learn about the weather condition for each state your driver will drive to and pass through before booking any load.

I recommend you use tools like weather.com or AccuWeather to monitor the weather. With these tools, you can check the weather hourly or for up to ten days, as this information is usually pretty accurate. You can also use the weather radar function to check live reports on weather conditions like snowfall in a particular area. This will help you determine if the conditions will end before your driver arrives.

Of course, you can use multiple resources, such as Google Maps, Trucker GPS, etc., to get information about the weather. But once you have enough information on the weather, you can then proceed to the next phase.

3. Traffic and time estimates

On a typical day and in perfect conditions, an average truck can go 60 miles per hour and up to 600 miles per day. It can even surpass that mileage if the driver is a professional. And on days with traffic and road closures, a truck may go around 500 miles daily.

Therefore, you want to check if there will be traffic and road closures, perhaps due to issues like fire, road construction, protests, riot, etc. You can check this on Google Maps, as the traffic option is available to see the live traffic feedback for a particular area.

Thus, it's best you map things out, even if it means getting a trucker's atlas, since it contains more details than normal road maps. For instance, a trucker's atlas will tell you which highways the driver will travel. That way, you'll be able to tell how many hours the journey will take and factor in your driver's HOS.

There are also dedicated state DOT websites that give this information in detail. For example, if you want to check lane closures in Texas, just Google "Texas, DOT traffic conditions," and you will find the specific website link for Texas DOT in Google's search results. In this case, it's https://its.txdot.gov

So, for instance, if a trip shows a 10-hour drive on Google Maps, don't assume it will be precisely 10 hours. Instead, you should add extra hours for traffic and other possible stops to create realistic time estimates.

4. Market conditions

Using the DAT freight and analytical tool, we can see the market conditions of a particular state regarding the number of loads going in and out of that state.

If a particular state has fewer loads going in but more loads going out, that's a **truck-less market**, resulting in more carrier rates per mile (carriers have the upper hand in negotiation here). But if a state has more loads going in and less going out, that's a **load-less market**, which means less rate per mile for carriers (where brokers have the upper hand in negotiation)

The DAT freight and analytical tool also provide more descriptive data on the Load vs. Trucks ratio. And you can easily select a state or market area to see the average loads and trucks.

For instance, you're in New York City and check the DAT freight and analytical tool to see if there are available loads. Luckily, it shows 430 loads are available and a truck count of 73 drivers. This means that once the 73 drivers are done loading, more than 350 loads will remain. Right?

So that's a truck-less market. And this is when you want to hit up brokers because you'll have the upper hand in negotiating, as they urgently need carriers at this point. And they won't be able to exploit you since you've already done a background check of the market to determine their conditions.

Generally, I like to see around 175 or more loads going out of an area. That's because getting a driver might be tricky if it's about 100 loads or less going out of an area. So if there are between 150 to at least 200 loads going out of an area, you have higher chances of finding loads and drivers too.

5. **Difficult areas, scales, and tolls**

Lastly, you also want to consider the difficult areas and those with scales and tolls along the route a driver will drive. Usually, most drivers like to go to the Midwest and South because these areas are easy.

It's hard to drive through places like Wyoming, Idaho, and Colorado, as most of these states require that the driver have chains. At the same time, some drivers don't like to deal with chains or don't know how to install them. Also, it's tough to drive through these areas during winter as the driver needs to know what they're doing and be willing to move the load there. Never try to push or force a driver to move loads to a destination they don't like to avoid unnecessary troubles.

Several places, like California, for instance, have many rules. Sometimes, I feel like they're in a different country on their own. For one, they have checklists that they use in checking whenever a driver comes in with a big truck. And they make sure to check everything and that a driver follows all their several rules. Some trucks don't even qualify to go to California, so you want to keep this in mind.

Arizona is an open area, as it has a vast desert area. For instance, you can drive for hours there and see nothing, which is why some drivers don't like going there. Meanwhile, there are other drivers who are just fine with this area, especially since they have high-speed limits. Regardless, I wouldn't recommend you let your driver drive too fast, especially when hauling significantly heavy loads.

Places like Oklahoma have many tolls, and getting out with a load can be difficult. However, Texas is okay, but loads coming out of here can be tricky and have low rates.

Whichever location your driver goes to, you must always check the scales and tolls to plan the number of hours the trip will take. And also, it's good for you to know the cost of these scales and tolls so that your broker doesn't take advantage of you when negotiating rates.

You can use Google Maps to find alternative routes if you want to avoid tolls. Google Map's data is pretty accurate.

Overall, trip planning is an excellent way to maximize your time and overcome all the obstacles you may encounter with moving loads. While it takes time to plan for every trip, eventually, you will become more productive in this stage of your trucking business.

Meanwhile, you should understand that having a one-fit-for-all policy regarding your schedule for booking loads is hard. For instance, if you have a driver that likes to move loads without stopping, you will book loads with tight schedules because you know they'll be on time or early. But if your driver likes to work with frequent breaks, you want to book loads with available pickup and delivery times, so they have enough time in between. Thus, you've got to be flexible with your trip planning.

6. TriHaul vs. Backhaul

Your job as an independent dispatcher doesn't end with booking a load; you must continually look for profitable loads for your carrier. And this is where the concept of TriHaul and backhaul kicks in.

Trust me, what I'm about to show you right now is a secret strategy that only the elite dispatchers know and use in finding loads that have a high rate per miles loads.

You see, what most dispatchers do whenever they get a load is to immediately start searching for the load back to their original destination (backhaul). But expert dispatchers know that this method usually has less rate per mile, which doesn't benefit their owner-operators either.

As a pro or elite dispatcher, you want to do things differently. And one way to do this is to apply the TriHaul strategy. Using a TriHaul tool like DAT's, you want to look for alternative lanes with shorter loads but much more rates per mile. For instance, let's say you picked up a load from point A to point B; instead of returning to A, you go to C first and then find a load from C to A.

Here's a good example using San Antonio, TX, Alabama, NY, and Fort Smith, AR:

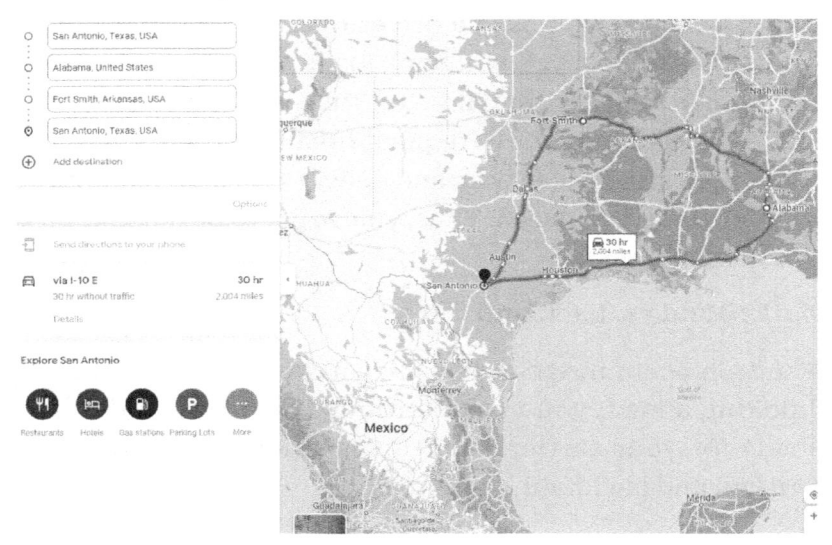

Usually, with the backhaul method, moving a load from San Antonio to Alabama under market conditions will cost around $1,500 for 825 miles, equaling $1.81 per mile.

However, applying the TriHaul strategy means you won't return to San Antonio. Instead, you want to find a load to haul from Alabama to a hot location, like Fort Smith in Arkansas, which has an excellent load-to-truck (L/T) ratio.

So let's say you move a load from Alabama to Fort Smith, which is around 627 miles for $2,500, at a rate of $3.98 per mile for a 10-hour drive.

You can see that the revenue is more than double what a driver who applied the backhauling method would get.

The best part is you can even find another load from Fort Smith, AR, to another hot location, like somewhere in Illinois or Georgia, and so on. So all you have to do is ensure that wherever you send your driver, there is always a reasonable rate for coming out of that area.

If market conditions are poor in one of your TriHaul locations, it is best to let them come out empty instead of hauling a heavy load for very low—good for a truck.

Although applying the TriHaul trick may look simple, it separates novice dispatchers from the pros and can increase revenue by 25%, 50%, or even 100%. It works.

Qualifying Process of Brokers

Another critical aspect you must pay attention to when finding loads is whether the broker is the right one and qualified enough. Unfortunately, not every broker has the proper setup for you. So you need to know the basics of finding the right one to succeed in the trucking business.

Of course, you could Google a broker's name to see if you can find any information about them. But I don't want you to pick a broker because they have a catchy company name or some great reviews online. No, that isn't the right way to do it!

I want to give you some insider knowledge to enable you to determine the right broker for you.

- **Check If the Broker Is Factorable**

You first want to do a credit check on the broker to ensure they're factorable. Recall we discussed what factoring companies are in Chapter 1.

If the broker isn't factorable, they may pay the factoring company late or not pay at all, which could make the factoring company refuse to work with the broker afterward.

So it's essential to check whether a broker is factorable or not. You also want to check whether the broker factors with your carrier's factoring company. And here is how to do it.

Using a paid service like TAFS, you can check whether the broker is listed under the "do not use list." If they are, it could mean they won't be able to pay the factoring company. Thus, your carrier will get a "chargeback" for the total load amount.

Let's say your carrier gets a load for $6,000, and they already have a chargeback of $2,000 from the previous load moved. This means the factoring company will deduct the $2,000 from their next payment and remit $4,000 only. This is what a chargeback is.

In the next chapter, I'll show you the role of factoring companies and how cash flow works in the trucking industry. You'll find this under the section **"Understand Billing and Invoicing the Right Way."**

- **Check the Broker's Credit**

Once you confirm your broker is factorable, the next thing is to check their credit score. Everyone has a credit score, and brokers are no exception, although theirs isn't based on their credit but on their ability and timely payments to their carriers.

So you want to check to see their credit score range. Generally, scores between 630 and 689 are fair, scores between 690 and 719 are considered good, and scores above 720 are excellent. However, scores below 630 are considered poor.

Here's how you can check your broker's credit:

- » *Use a third-party service:* While you can perform a free credit check at your convenience, thanks to the many factoring companies and load boards that offer this service, you can also perform a credit check on a broker using a third-party service like FMCSA or Ansonia. The best way to do this is to enter the broker's information and check their credit history from the result. You should also confirm that the broker's license is still intact.

- » *Ask questions:* You should ask other dispatchers and carriers to know if they've ever hauled any load for the broker you intend to work with. And they'll give you honest feedback in most cases.

- » *Trust your instincts:* Yes, you must always trust your instincts. Once you feel that a broker isn't straightforward with you or trying to misinform you, you should trust your gut and avoid them altogether.

Of course, you wouldn't want to book a load with a broker with a low credit score because the chances of them not paying your carrier are higher. When I encounter such brokers, I take to my heels as I don't want to waste my time, energy, and fuel moving a load and getting screwed at the end.

Before You Start Negotiating Rates with Brokers

So you've finally found a load that meets your needs, but are you getting the best rate you can get for it?

Before accepting any load, you want to avoid settling for an introductory rate, which is where negotiation comes in, so you must prepare yourself for this. And there is a lot of information you want to focus on to enable you to negotiate the best rate effectively. So let's check them out:

- **Confirm Load Details**

    » *The number of miles:* How many miles is your driver driving? Are they doing a rate per mile or just from the state line to the state line? These are the questions you want to answer, as it plays a part in your rate negotiation. You may have calculated the specific miles from the driver's origin to the destination and be 40 or 50 miles short. Meanwhile, your broker already agreed on a fixed rate based on state line to state line. As a result, you'll run into issues. So make sure you consider the number of miles.

    » *The number of stops:* The haulage could have multiple stops, such as one pickup spot and maybe three or four drop-off spots. It could also be a single pickup and drop-off spot. So you want to consider this factor to enable you to negotiate better rates with the broker. For instance, if the haulage has multi-stops or drop-offs, you can tell the broker to pay an additional $50 per drop-off and calculate the total cost at the final drop-off spot.

» *Deadhead miles:* Also known as "empty miles," it's the distance between when a truck driver delivers a load and drives to the following pickup location with an empty load. For instance, if it's 100 miles of deadhead miles, that'll cost a lot of gas money. Thus, you want to inform your broker about it so they can pay, even if it's just half payment.

» *Time of pickup and delivery:* You want to discuss the time of pickup and delivery, depending on your driver's HOS and work activity.

» *Weight of the load:* Knowing the freight's weight is very important because the heavier the load, the more wear and tear you'll do to your driver's truck. So if the load weighs more, you have to negotiate with the broker to pay more. And when I say "weighs more," I'm referring to a load weighing around 40,000 lbs, which is considerably heavier than the usual 15,000 lbs to 20,000 lbs load weight for a 53-foot truck. Imagine what would happen if a truck went up the mountains with such a heavy load. And if it's during the hot season, the truck's tire may get damaged more easily, so you want to consider all of these factors.

» *Tolls:* You should check for tolls along the route your driver will move a load and try to estimate the total cost. That way, you'll have an idea of what rate to negotiate with the broker.

Sometimes, you might have already agreed on the load's weight and rate with the broker. But when your driver reaches there, they find out the load weighs more than what was paid for. So what do you do in this situation?

You should check the load's weight to see if the truck can carry it conveniently. If it does, then that's great. What you want to do next is call the broker to inform them about the new weight and negotiate with them to pay more money.

However, if the load weight is something the truck can't carry, or the driver loads and scales the truck only to see it's overweight, you want to avoid such haulage. So call your broker and forward the receipts or proof your driver sent you. Tell them you're overweight and need to cut the load because if the driver goes through a scale house and is over his maximum weight, they'll get to book them a ticket or even shut them down in some cases. And you wouldn't want that to happen, right?

Accessorial & Carrier Fees

Accessorial fees are the compensation a carrier expects for anything other than the standard pickup and delivery operation. Below are some things you want to look out for as far as accessorial fees are concerned:

- **Layover fee:** Let's assume you're pulling for Walmart, which sometimes gets overbooked in delivery. So your driver arrives there on time for his delivery, but Walmart couldn't receive the driver at a specific time. So they have to lay over to the next day or for the next available appointment. In this case, you want to get that additional fee for your driver. Some companies pay around $250 for layover fees.

- **Lumper fee:** This is the fee you or your driver must pay to get the freight off the truck. You wouldn't expect your driver to do the offloading or pay the fee from their pocket. So that's when you call the broker and tell them the driver has arrived at the destination and needs a lumper fee. (Lumper fee is usually around $200.)

- **Driver assist fee (load and unload pay):** The carrier charges this amount if they have to assist with loading or unloading the load. This charge becomes a part of a shipment if the driver's labor is needed to load or unload the freight from their truck.

- **TONU (Truck Order Not Used) fee:** Let's say a driver arrives at the shipper's destination, and the shipper doesn't have the load ready for pickup, or they've already put it on another truck; you have to compensate your driver because their time is valuable. They should be paid for arriving to pick up that load, and that's when you can ask for a TONU fee.

- **Detention fee:** Asking for this fee can be tricky, as some brokers don't like to pay the driver the detention fee. However, the driver gets compensated with this fee if they arrive at the destination and don't get offloaded within the two-hour window. The detention fee is an hourly compensation fee.

- **Tarp, straps, blankets, and binders:** This is the amount the carrier charges for the laborious act of tarping a load or using straps, blankets, and binders. This fee comes into play, especially when flat beds are involved. Generally, your driver needs to get these items to secure the load firmly to the truck, so it doesn't move about while in transit.

- **Extra stops:** Sometimes, a broker may add extra stops

to the routine stops a load had initially started with. As a result, carriers can charge extra fees for these extra stops, as hauling the load would now take more time and fuel.

- **Claim:** This is the recovery process from a carrier and their insurance underwriter for excessive charges, loss, or damage to the load, delay in delivery, etc.
- **Fuel surcharges:** Extra compensation a carrier gets when fuel prices increase.

Your carrier may also request some other form of compensation in addition to just driving. So talk to them, make sure you negotiate, and, most importantly, put all the procedures and fees paid in writing.

Your Fee As A Dispatcher

While you want to be competitive with your rate, you also want to ensure you charge your worth. But try not to overcharge for your service. For instance, you can start off as a new dispatcher with a rate of 6% or 7% per load. I wouldn't focus on charging ridiculous rates starting, and I wouldn't charge too low.

Time and again, I see desperate dispatchers charging 2% or 3%, and their carriers laugh at them. I'm not saying that carriers don't use them, but those are the ones carriers are likely to try to run all over.

So how do you know the correct rate to charge your carrier? Well, here's an illustration:

Let's say you fix your rate at 6%, your carrier wants $3.00 per mile, and you find them a load from Texas to Atlanta 800 loaded miles with a posted rate of $2,000. You'll have to request $2,400 (multiply the per-mile rate and loaded miles) from the broker.

Calculating your 6% will be $2,400x 6%, which equals $144.

So, whatever you do, you want to negotiate at least $2,544 to ensure your carrier gets what he needs per mile, and you get your fee too.

Calling Brokers & Rate Negotiation

Now here comes the calling and negotiation part. Of course, based on our previous lessons, you know by now that you have to negotiate to get the best rate.

If you call your broker to negotiate a rate, you want to ensure that you have specific information handy. You should grab your pen and paper and note down the following:
- Driver's name and cell phone number
- Carrier's MC/DOT numbers
- Truck and trailer numbers
- An idea of the rate you have in mind (and why)
- The driver's current location
- The pickup and delivery times and dates—confirm if they're fixed or open
- What type of load it is—ask for details about moving freight
- How much does the load weigh
- Deadhead miles
- Number of stops
- Ask about any needed supplies, including things like a tarp, straps, blankets, and binders

The load rate confirmation sheet also serves as the rate and load information/confirmation for your carriers. Therefore, you need it for every load you haul. I have also provided a filled-in sample to give you an idea of a load rate confirmation sheet.

Once you call and start negotiating your rates, ensure every agreement is always in writing and effect your rate confirmation. You also want to ensure that before signing the rate confirmation on behalf of your owner-operator or your carrier, everything you negotiated on the telephone is listed on that rate confirmation sheet. Finally, once you gather all these details, you have all you need to call and negotiate with your brokers.

I know it's a lot of work. And I won't lie to you— finding loads for trucks is one of the hardest yet most crucial aspects of running a freight dispatch business. It was stressful when I started, as I had nobody to guide me. Sometimes, I had to Google my way through. Then, other times, I had to figure things out myself. It's a roller coaster experience I don't want you to experience.

So I encourage you to do your homework and follow my advice to avoid disappointing the people you'll be working with and giving yourself unnecessary headaches.

Load Board Video Tutorial w/ Live Examples

To make the whole process a breeze, I have prepared a live walkthrough video with examples so you can better understand how a load board works and how to use it to find a load. You'll also learn how to do proper trip planning from the video guide.

All you need to do is **click the bonuses link at the beginning of the guide and find the resource listed under Free**

Bonus#11.

What Is a Carrier Packet?

To speed up carrier setup and assist in approving them to transport freight, brokers submit a package containing several documents. Then, the carrier gives the broker the completed contracts and paperwork back. Each carrier packet contains the same forms and agreements.

As a dispatcher, you will be responsible for completing all carrier packets, and you only need to fill it out once for each broker. However, suppose an essential form or contract is missing from the carrier packet. In that case, you won't have all the information you need to onboard carriers, inform them of your expectations, and comply with regulatory bodies.

Now, you don't want your carrier having to pull over to fill out carrier packets so they can get a load. That's your responsibility, and you want to ensure that you promptly get the carrier packets across to the brokers.

Remember that one carrier packet is needed per broker, so once you fill it out, you never have to do it again. So, for instance, if you signed a carrier packet with Walmart in 2018 or 2019, you never have to do it again. The only thing you have to do is update the insurance certificate with them annually.

Below are the details you'll need to fill a carrier packet correctly:

- **Carrier profile:** The carrier's name, address, contact information, MC & DOT numbers
- **Copy of the carrier's authority (MC authority document):**

The carrier registers their authority with FMCSA, so they get this certificate, typically called an authority document. It will show the MC and DOT number and the date it is granted.

- **Notice of Assignment (NOA):** If the client factors, which they usually do, you'll need the contact information of the factoring company.

- **Payment information:** This is for mailing payments or banking info for direct deposit.

- **Signed and initiated broker-carrier agreement:** You will have to sign on behalf of your carrier since you are acting as an authorized representative of the carrier, so under signature, you can put your signature and sign it by the designation of "manager."

- **W-9 Form:** The W-9 form is filled by the carrier, but the broker needs to obtain it because they need to send it to the IRS to tell how much they paid the carrier that year.

- **Proof of insurance (certificate of insurance -COI):** You get this from the insurance carrier, usually liability insurance and cargo insurance. Some brokers may also need equipment numbers of insured items listed in the form. You must have proof of insurance and do your due diligence to ensure the insurance certificate is valid. I have seen cases where carriers faked their certificates, which will cost you in the long run if you don't check earlier. So ensure to validate everything your carrier sends to you.

Once you have all these details, you can proceed to fill out the carrier packet. I'll use the TQL Carrier Packet as a case study for this illustration. **You can also open the filled-in**

sample in the resources folder to follow along given under Free Bonus# 3.

On the first page of the carrier packet, you'll find the company profile sheet, which tells every detail about the broker's company, including its name, address, banking, references, and other important information.

The second page is the carrier form. Make sure you read every instruction written. Then go ahead and enter the requested details, which include the following:

- **Carrier's name:** Write the carrier's company name in full and clarify if it's an LLC or INC.

- **Dispatchers:** You put your name or dispatcher company's name and possibly your phone number here if there isn't a separate space.

- **Address:** Enter the carrier's company address.

- **Phone number:** Enter the carrier's company phone number

- **Email Address:** As a dispatcher, you can put your email address here so they can email you directly.

- Enter every other information requested.

The third page is the payment terms. Here, you'll have to indicate which payment term you would like to use. These are the available payment options:

- **28-Day Pay:** There are no fees involved.

- **7-Day Quick Pay:** TQL will charge a 3% fee from the gross truck rate.

- **1-Day Quick Pay:** TQL will charge a 3% fee from the gross truck rate. Also, payment is made with either a Comcheck, which includes a $25 per invoice Comcheck fee, or direct deposit with no Comcheck fee.

But I recommend you avoid the quick pay option if the company you're moving a load for is factoring. For example, let's say your carrier needs a 1-Day Quick Pay, and the client is factoring and is paying only $3,000 for the shipment; that means you'll get only $2,825 after deducting the 3% service and $25 Comcheck fee. You wouldn't want that, right?

Also, do understand that whatever selection you make here will remain as the permanent payment term until the carrier services are notified in writing about the changes.

The fourth page is the Comcheck Authorization. You should note if you would like to limit who at your company is permitted to receive Comchecks. So do mark the appropriate "Yes" or "No" option.

The fifth page is the Direct Deposit Agreement, Change and Cancellation Form, and Authorization Agreement. So you want to go through it and fill it out appropriately.

The sixth page is the Substitute W-9 Form. For instance, TQL uses this form to decide whether to file Form 1099-MISC yearly for a payee.

The IRS requires that TQL provide their payees with the standard federal W-9 form or our substitute W-9 form to hold in the payee's file. So read through and complete the requested information as requested.

The seventh-fourteenth pages are the broker/carrier agreement. Again, it's pretty long, so you must read it carefully before signing.

The fifteenth page, which happens to be the last, is an appendix for additional requirements regarding hazardous materials and waste shipments.

While filling out the carrier packet, ensure you enter every information correctly, provide all the necessary documents requested, and adhere to every written instruction on each carrier packet page to get approved faster. You should attach the carrier's MC authority, NOA (for factoring), and COI documents on submission. Also, ensure you read through the agreement and do not just sign any dotted line you see without understanding what that part means.

One more thing; there is no fee required to fill a carrier packet. So anyone who demands payment before completing the form or during submission is probably a scammer attempting to take advantage of your ignorance.

The only costs you might incur are those related to a letter of insurance, which is a record of a carrier's history as an insured driver, or a PDF editor subscription. However, there are numerous free online PDF editor programs available.

And that brings us to the end of this chapter. I know this whole process sounds like so much work, but it's a small price to pay for having an effective load search strategy, don't you think? Of course, even with a good strategy, searching for loads might still take some time. However, your load search time and the stress involved will gradually reduce. Then, as you connect with more reliable brokers, dispatchers, and carriers, you'll start making waves in your trucking business effortlessly.

Key Takeaway

1. Load boards are online matching services that connect shippers to brokers and brokers to carriers or transport owners.

2. As a dispatcher, the best way to boost profitability is to find the highest-paying loads and best freight routes.

3. Not every broker has the proper setup for you, so when finding loads, check whether the broker is the right one and qualified enough.

4. Accessorial fees are the compensation a carrier expects for anything other than the standard pickup and delivery operation.

5. As a dispatcher, you will be responsible for completing all carrier packets. You only need to fill it out once for each broker.

CHAPTER 5

TRACKING LOADS AND FINAL WORKFLOW

"Every problem is a gift—without problems, we would not grow."
— *Anthony Robbins*

HONESTLY, WORKING AS an independent dispatcher might require long, intense workdays. While on duty, you're in charge of all communications and scheduling of trips and drivers. These communications may include information about traffic delays, vehicle breakdowns, project delays, or delivery problems.

In addition, you're in charge of keeping track of transportation costs such as fuel consumption, repairs, and maintenance. You're also responsible for recording all freight shipment and delivery information and planning routes that will ultimately save your carrier money and your driver time. And depending on the size of your dispatching business, you'll find yourself checking and ensuring the accuracy of completed timesheets, payroll, and other essential documents.

Generally, your work as an independent dispatcher involves

several processes. And that's why you must stay focused and organized, communicate effectively, pay attention to detail, and have a good workflow. Fortunately, I've put this chapter together to guide you in simplifying the everyday processes you'll engage in as an independent dispatcher.

Typical Day of a Truck Dispatcher

So what's the typical day-to-day routine of a truck dispatching business owner like?

Well, I start the day by completing my morning rituals once I wake. Then, I make sure I'm ready to start finding loads latest by 8 a.m., as the best time to book loads is between 7 a.m. and 10 a.m. So you want to ensure you always wake up early and prepare for the day.

You also have to consider your time zone, as your brokers, carriers, and owner-operators may be in a different time zone. Although in the US, most of those you would work with use the eastern time zone. So it's always a good idea to get up early and start finding loads; after all, that's what keeps the business going.

I usually start working on my invoices around 10 or 11 a.m. (I have to send invoices for whatever load I move in a day). Although sometimes you may wait two to three days before sending, it's usually a good idea to send an invoice or invoices daily.

So let's say you've got four trucks, each delivering a load; you'll be sending invoices for the day, but that shouldn't take more than 30 minutes. So I recommend you get it done ASAP rather than pile them up. But, of course, the best part of sending invoices early is getting paid faster, especially if your client uses a factoring company, and they usually do.

Daily Goals and Challenges to Expect

In addition to your regular day-to-day routine, as an independent dispatcher, you'll also be responsible for helping with load issues. As with other businesses, you will often face issues and situations you didn't plan for. It could be a severe issue, such as your carrier getting shut down or the truck breaking down, or a minor issue, like the driver delivering the load to the wrong address or having a dispute with someone at the warehouse.

Issues like these frequently happen, so you must brace yourself and be ready. You'll have to stop every other thing you're doing and step in as the dispatcher to resolve the problem. And if necessary, don't hesitate to contact every involved party. You see, while the carrier's primary goal is to keep their wheels on the road, it's your duty as the dispatcher to ensure everything else is in compliance.

Support You Need to Give

No, I'm not referring to the kind of support of an 8 to 5 job here, as such a schedule won't work for the dispatching business.

For instance, I dispatch for three flatbeds and two reefers, and I can tell you I hardly get a lot of sleep. And that's because the people I work with call me so often. Even when facing minor issues they can resolve themselves, they would still call me for assistance, perhaps, because they know I'm available or are just a bit lazy. Sometimes, it feels like I'm babysitting them.

So you have to be mindful of how you do things. Sometimes, you'll have to listen to the issues of the people you work with and walk them through simple solutions.

And aside from helping your carriers with load issues, you also want to help them scale their business. For instance, if you have a carrier with one truck, you want to intentionally help them to go from one truck to two trucks, especially if that's their goal. You can as well help get a driver for the truck. That way, you will help your carrier make more money, and you, as the dispatcher, and your broker will make more money too. That's a win-win situation, isn't it?

Tracking Your Loads and Carriers

Now that we've covered a typical day for a truck dispatcher let's get into more practical and operational tips on tracking your loads and carriers.

1. Using Software

Many trucking companies use software to track and match loads with trucks to haul them, and you can do the same. But to be more efficient at your job, you must learn how the software works and how to use it exceptionally. You may need to explore and read about the software during your leisure to know the best ways to integrate it with your job. Here are the software programs I recommend you use:

- **Ascend TMS:** Ascend TMS is a decent TMS (transport management system) you can use and has a free basic plan. Of course, several training tutorials on YouTube cover detailed information on using Ascend TMS, so feel free to check them out.

- **TruckingOffice:** You can also opt for TruckingOffice, especially as it's a good option for small dispatching companies managing 20 trucks or less.
- **Square:** Although Square is mainly used to fulfill sales transactions, you can also use it as a TMS.

2. **Using Spreadsheets**

Another way to track loads and carriers is by making use of spreadsheets. They'll help you stay organized and track all your truck schedules, gross amounts, profits and expenses, the equipment used, driver information, and broker contacts. Although spreadsheets look simple, they're effective for tracking.

I strongly recommend that you use Google Spreadsheets. And if you don't have a Google account, go to https://google.com and create a free account. **I've made a template available to get you to track immediately; please find the "All-in-One Dispatch Management Spreadsheet" listed under Free bonuses #4, 5, 6, and make a copy for yourself. I've also prepared a live walkthrough video on how to use this spreadsheet in your dispatch workflow. So do check it out too.**

Once you start using this template, it'll automatically be saved in your Google Drive and Google Sheets accounts. You want to bookmark that address so that you can access it anytime from any of your devices. You can even share it with your team members and allow them to make changes, which will sync across all users' devices.

Understand Billing and Invoicing the Right Way

Another activity you'll find yourself doing frequently is preparing the billing and sending invoices to your clients. And there are two types of invoices you want to focus on here. One is for your carrier so that they can get paid, while the other invoice is for your services to the carrier so you can get paid. **Meanwhile, I've added excel templates for both kinds of invoices inside the Free Bonus #2 to give you an idea of what they look like.** Now, let's examine these two cases closely.

- **How Does the Carrier Get Paid?**

So here's how the cash collection process typically works in the trucking industry.

Once your driver delivers a load for your broker, you've fulfilled your part of the agreement, and now it's time for you to get paid. So what you need to do is email or fax the invoice to the broker along with the necessary paperwork, including your load confirmation, your proof of delivery, your BOL, and accessorial and carrier fee receipts.

Once you do that, the carrier typically has to wait 30 to 90 days before the broker can pay them. For a small business owner like you, that can be very detrimental to your cash flow. But that's where the factoring company comes in, and we've already discussed how it works in Chapters 1 and 4.

So instead of waiting for 30 to 90 days, a factoring company will pay the money in advance to the carrier, usually within 24 to 48 hours.

Now, as a dispatcher, you'll be responsible for submitting the paperwork for payment to the factoring company. Just log onto the factoring company's portal, enter all the necessary information, and upload documents like the load confirmation sheet, BOL, POD, etc. Then hit the "Save Invoice" button and wait to see that it's already processing because, in some cases, you may have missed some aspects that need your attention.

- **How You Get Paid as Dispatcher**

Now, if you're wondering how and when to ask for your payment, in my experience, you should bill or charge your clients right away for the services you've provided. After all, your accountant charges you for tax preparation when you get your taxes done. So you should do the same; you've done a service, and now you're billing or charging your client to get paid. It's that simple!

You can do this the good old way by sending out an invoice to your client, but this method has a big flaw, as you may not get paid while still providing a dispatching service to a client.

In this case, I recommend you use a more modern version of invoicing, which is sending out a digital invoice to your client via email. So all they have to do is click on the link and make the payment. That way, you'll immediately know if they've paid or not. There are several apps you can use to send a digital invoice. I use PayPal, as it's easy to use and allows me to create and send my carrier an invoice directly with no monthly fees. Other applications you can use are Zelle, Square, and Cashapp.

Sometimes, a client may refuse to pay, so it's important that you screen your carriers and build a working business relationship with them. Also, you must offer an excellent customer service experience so that they don't have a reason not to pay or to look for another dispatcher. But for those cases where the carrier doesn't pay, here are the things you can do:

First, contact the carrier as soon as possible to know if they have a valid reason for the overdue payment, like a complaint. Usually, a brief phone conversation can put things in perspective and allow you to start formulating a solution.

After your conversation, even if the carrier is unwilling to pay the invoice, you'll have the necessary information to decide what to do next. However, things can become trickier when the carrier refuses to pay for different reasons.

You'll probably never get the entire amount you're owed if the carrier has gone out of business. If the carrier declares bankruptcy, there is a slim chance that they will eventually pay you. Even if they promise to pay at least part of the payment when they sell their assets, this process could take years. And there is no guarantee you'll get paid since you probably are one of many waiting for your money.

Carriers that disregard your calls and bills might not have any intention of paying, at least not right away. If the bill is huge, you could sue the carrier or send the invoice to a collection agency for further assistance.

You may file a claim if a carrier doesn't pay after a reasonable or agreed-upon amount of time. Contracts frequently specify 30, 60, or 90 days following delivery.

However, there are some of the measures you can take as a

dispatcher to prevent non-payment of your invoices:

It's essential to communicate all facts in writing from the beginning with the carrier. Always be upfront about any potential accessorial costs and other carrier fees by keeping the lines of communication open.

Make sure to document everything and organize your documents. You may manage your load documentation and streamline the payment procedure by using a specific folder.

You can charge upfront if you decide to work with the carrier next time.

You can also include in your agreement that you will charge an additional fee for late payments.

Workflow of Dispatching

Okay, so let's talk about the final workflow of the whole dispatching process. However, before we get right into it, let's define the term "workflow."

A workflow is a series of steps through which a task progresses from initiation to completion. When we apply that to our dispatching business, you'll see it's pretty much the same. The dispatching workflow is the sequence of outlined steps a dispatcher must follow to get the dispatching job done.

It involves getting the carrier to sign the dispatch agreement and send it back to you and following that process until you've received the payment for the load that you've booked for them.

To make your learning curve easy and understand the steps involved in the truck dispatching business faster, I have shared a sample of my workflow below.

So let's get right into it.

Step 1: Finding a Carrier and Getting Them Signed

The first thing to do is to find a carrier and note down their information, including their equipment type, what kind of load they want to move, the location, where they would like to go, and all other necessary details.

Once you have all the information about the carrier, send them the dispatch service agreement for them to sign. And that's it!

Of course, you should keep a copy of the signed dispatch service agreement in your records for future reference.

Step 2: Finding a Load and Trip Planning

The next step is to find a load. Since you already have your carrier or owner-operator's details, you should have a better idea of the kind of load to look for. But first, before you start searching for a load, you want to confirm your driver's HOS and availability. Then you can search loads using software like DAT Power by entering your carrier's details. Once you find a load that interests you, you need to do proper trip planning and ensure everything is in place. But to do this, you need to check
- Rate per mile for the total trip miles;
- Weather conditions of the trip;
- Traffic and time estimates for the route the driver will follow;
- Market conditions of the area;
- Difficult areas with traffic and tolls; and

- Availability of additional loads from the destination of the first load.

Once you're done with your market research, you can proceed with calling the broker.

Step 3: Booking the Load and Completing the Paperwork

The third step is to contact the broker associated with the load you need to book for your carrier. The broker would ask you for the MC or USDOT number to verify the carrier. And this is where you need to do the rate negotiation and paperwork if you get the load.

If the broker doesn't have the carrier signed up to their platform yet, they will send you a carrier packet to complete and return. As I already explained, the carrier packet is a form or collection of documents the broker will use to facilitate the carrier setup and approve them to haul the load.

Although sometimes the carrier may have filled the carrier packet with the broker directly, you should ask for a copy for future reference—especially if you'll be booking many loads for the carrier with different brokers. That way, you'll have their information handy and help set them up with new brokers.

Once the broker receives the filled carrier packet, they will send a load and rate confirmation sheet to the carrier or dispatcher for signing. As a dispatcher, read the load and rate confirmation sheet thoroughly, confirm that all the details are correct, and agree with the load specifications. Once you confirm this, sign the document on behalf of your carrier and email the copy to your carrier.

However, if you check and notice that some details on the load and rate confirmation sheet aren't correct or do not agree with the load specifications, then do not hesitate to contact the broker to clarify the issue. You should pay attention to details here, so the broker doesn't exploit you.

Step 4: Dispatch and Watch the Load Until It's Delivered

After completing all the paperwork, it's finally time to dispatch. So you tell your driver to get the load and ask your broker to release the load to them.

At this stage, follow through with the load by keeping in touch with your driver. That way, you'll know when they arrive at the pickup location and when they reach the delivery destination.

You should also encourage them to contact you and the broker when they encounter any issues.

Step 5: Upload Invoices to the Factoring Company or Send them to the broker.

Once you've confirmed that your driver has delivered the load to the correct destination, it's time to sort out the billing and invoicing. First, you'll need to prepare an invoice for your payment and email it directly to your broker or the factoring company so your carrier can get paid on time. Always remember to attach the BOL, POD, and signed load and rate confirmation sheet in the email.

Step 6: Send Invoices to Carrier for Your Dispatching Charges (Usually Weekly)

Finally, you should prepare an invoice for your dispatching charges and send it to the carrier so you can get paid too.

Although you could do this weekly, I recommend you send your invoice to the carrier immediately after the shipment process is completed and send an invoice to the factoring company or broker for them to get paid.

As you can see, all of these steps sum up the high-level dispatching workflow. Although it looks very much like a summary or an overview, you'll discover that it becomes more engaging the moment you get started. But try to keep things organized; you can get through these steps before you know it.

Key Takeaway

1. In addition to your regular day-to-day routine, as an independent dispatcher, you'll also be responsible for helping with load issues.

2. Aside from helping your carriers with load issues, you also want to help them scale their business.

3. You can use software or spreadsheets to track and match loads with trucks to haul them.

4. The two types of invoices you want to pay attention to are the ones you send to the broker or upload to the factoring company's platform so your carrier can get paid and the ones you send to the carrier so you can get paid.

5. You need to have a dispatching workflow, a series of steps you must follow to get the dispatching job done.

CHAPTER 6

SCALING YOUR BUSINESS

"You only have to do a few things right in your life so long as you don't do too many things wrong."

— Warren Buffet

FINALLY, YOU'RE AT that stage where you need to wrap everything you've learned so far and see how you can take your dispatching business to the next level.

You need to understand that running a business differs from scaling and taking the business to the next level. For instance, let's say you've just set up your dispatching business. Without a defined plan for scaling your business, you may mistake the business as a success simply because it achieved massive growth quickly. But the truth is that when a business or company expands very quickly, it opens itself up to several issues because there needs to be a solid plan to support rapid growth. And you don't want that to happen to your dispatching business, right?

One way to reduce your chances of facing these issues is to learn how to scale your dispatching business. Ultimately, as you learn how to scale your trucking business, you will create foundational procedures to support your business's growth in the long term.

Before scaling your business, it's essential to consider what it means to establish a business. For instance, you started your dispatching business to solve the problems in the trucking industry and increase your income. Now, you need to grow your dispatching business to keep it profitable and reach more clients in the trucking industry. And to do so, you must put systems and procedures into place to prepare you for consistent, profitable development.

Building Your Brand

Trust me, a well-known brand that its customers love is one of the best assets you could ever have. But, as a small dispatching business, you may compete against big trucking players with devoted clients and substantial marketing budgets. So you must find ways to build your brand and make it stand out from the crowd. When you do this, you'll scale your business in the long term.

So, how do you build a brand?

Have a Mind Shift from Solo Player to A Business

One critical decision to move the needle in your dispatching business is to stop trying to do the one-person show and make yourself a real business instead. You can't continue to work from your home's basement and dispatch loads thinking you'll make a billion-dollar trucking business; that just doesn't work.

You've got to break that mentality of making a quick buck or achieving quick success overnight without putting a proper plan in place. Of course, you may get a few owner-operators, but not much else. So you must stop playing the solo game and start thinking instead . . .

"How do I establish myself as a business?"

"How do I build my brand?"

Establishing yourself as a brand means more than just creating a fancy website or designing a nice logo. No! It's much more than that. You've got to have the proper structure with the right offer for your dispatching business and not just live off the load board all the time.

Make It Easy to Choose You

Your business's success depends on your customers, so you need to make them positively engage with your brand. The whole point is to find ways to consistently show them you have their best interests at heart so they can always choose you. Here's how to make it easy for your clients to choose you:

- **Craft your USP**

Knowing your USP (unique selling proposition) will help you answer the question, "Why should clients work with you?" If you're just selling—that is, always finding, booking, and dispatching loads—you'll only be making noise out there. This is because 90% of independent dispatchers are doing the same thing—they're just selling, so you want to stand out from them.

One way to do this is to look at what other dispatchers are doing, find their weaknesses, and use your story and voice to project why you're different.

- **Have introductory front-end offers**

As the name implies, introductory front-end offers come before back-end offers. When marketing, you want to make your front-end offers more affordable to attract more clients to whom you can later sell your back-end services.

Introductory front-end offers include offering discounts for a week or two or a month or making your clients' first two loads free. It all depends on your marketing goal. That way, your clients will feel like they're saving money and want to work with you. Then later, you can slowly increase your rates.

- **Craft compelling offers with back-end services**

Once you have good introductory front-end offers and you set it right, the next thing you should do is craft compelling back-end offers. Trust me; this is where the money is. But you've got to think like a marketer here. So here are some back-end services you can incorporate into your dispatching business:

» *Marketing and sales services:* You can help your carriers generate more leads through shippers or distribution centers. You can also offer your team's services to call those leads and convert them to paying customers on their behalf. Finally, you can help influence and negotiate with shippers, close deals for carriers, and build long-term relationships.

» *Operations services:* Many owner-operators run a one-person show. If you can make them understand the importance of building a team and setting up processes, you will easily win them over. You can do this by offering your managerial services and doing various tasks for them, like

- » *Helping* them find new drivers;
- » *Guiding* them in buying new trucks to grow their fleet;
- » *Hiring* and training dispatchers who could work for them; and
- » *Offering* them discounted repair maintenance services for their trucks.
- » *Accounting services:* Accounting services are crucial in the trucking industry, but many carriers and owner-operators find it challenging to execute effective accounts. So if you can do this well, you may want to help them out by offering the following accounting services:
- » *Services* geared toward beneficial tax
- » *Full* compliance at all times
- » *A business* willing to leverage opportunities to grow
- » *A seamless,* more affordable way of running the business
- » *Taking care* of various renewals, like insurance, licenses, and medical cards of their drivers
- » *Taking care* of IFTA quarterly fuel report
- » *Factoring* Service

With all your clients' accounting accounts in order, you can make them feel safe knowing that their business is running well, complies with regulatory bodies, and has opportunities for future growth.

All these small things will stack up to make your back-end offer better and make you more money in the long term. As time passes, you'll no longer be an average joe sitting in their basement, trying to make a couple of bucks off the load board. Instead, you'll become a truck-dispatching magnate.

Have an Online Presence

You have more options to increase your brand's recognition and boost your reputation when you have more ways to promote your dispatching business to your target audience and provide them with exceptional experiences. And having an online presence is a great way to reach your target audience and stand out from competitors. But how do you build a good online presence?

- **Create a logo:** You should create a logo for your dispatching business. I always find talents on Upwork to design my logos, but you can also use Fiverr. **I have included some done-for-you canva templates for logos, social media pages, business cards, and flyers. Please check the free bonuses #7,8,9,&10**

- **Create social media pages:** You can use social media platforms like Facebook, Twitter, Instagram, and YouTube to create a page for your dispatching business and build a following. But try not to spread yourself too thin across every social media platform; instead, leverage the few ones most suitable for your business.

- **Have a business address:** You can get a virtual address if you want to add your business on Google and your business cards. I pay $9.99 per month with ipostal.com, but it's something that can wait if needed.

- **Register for a Google Business Profile:** This works very well in places like the United States, so don't hesitate to register your dispatching business with Google Business Profile. After all, setting up a profile is free. You should tell those you work with to leave reviews so that others can see that your dispatching services are excellent.

- **Have a phone number:** You want a business phone number or a Google number so that carriers don't call your private line. However, you can skip this idea if you prefer to use your private line. Though if you choose to do that, I would recommend you have a professional voicemail and be sure to answer all calls in case the caller is your carrier, broker, or receiver.

- **Create a professional website:** You should register a domain name, like www.dispatcherjoe.com, with a domain registrar, like Google Domains or Namecheap. Then, set up a website yourself; you can use Vistaprint, Squarespace, or WordPress. You can also hire an expert on micro-job platforms, like Fiverr and Upwork, and get it done under as low as $50. Whatever you do, always ensure the content on your website is of high quality and promotes your USP.

- **Get a professional email:** Although this idea is optional, it can easily make you stand out. Now, instead of just using a gmail.com or yahoo.com extension, you can have a professional email with your domain name, such as contact@dispatcherjoe.com. Almost all domain name providers offer this service, so do check it out.

- **Business cards and flyers:** You want to design business cards and flyers for your business. When designing flyers, you must make sure you mention your USP clearly and that the design is legible and nice enough to stand out from the crowd.

Different Ways of Finding A Carrier

In Chapter 3, we discussed how to go about getting your first carrier. And if you can remember, I promised to show you in great detail how to leverage various online and offline methods to find carriers.

So consider this section as an extension of chapter 3. Here, we'll look at two primary ways you can find a carrier—the online and offline methods.

1. **Online Methods of Finding a Carrier**

- **Through load boards**

The focus is to search trucks on load boards like DAT Power for small businesses with maybe only one truck or new carrier businesses that are about to launch in the upcoming weeks.

Usually, these carriers need help, so you could just call them and pitch your dispatching services to them. The advantage of this method is you know that they'll always need a load since they're just starting.

Even if they haven't started yet, that is—they don't need a load right away but are looking to start in the next few days or weeks—you can still talk to them. And if interested in working with you, you can follow up and ask them when they're planning to start. That way, you'll know when they are ready to start and need a load.

- **Trucking authority directories**

To find new carriers, you can use trucking authority directories like DAT directory, Partner Carrier, Quick Transport

Solutions, and CarrierSource. These directories allow you to look for carriers based on defined categories like their states and cities. You can also use FMCSA to find new and existing carriers.

The FMCSA website is handy for you as a dispatcher. It helped me when I started, too, as I could find carriers listed in alphabetical order with further details like their states, cities, and contact information.

- **Utilizing job boards**

You can also use job boards like Craigslist, Indeed, Monster, Career Builder, and Ziprecruiter to find new carriers. You can post an ad on these job boards showing that you're looking for owner-operators and drivers for your dispatch business or simply looking for a job as a dispatcher.

Many owner-operators and drivers use these platforms regularly, so you should consider it too. You can make a new post three times a week and continue to renew the posts as many times as possible.

- **Social Media**

Aside from creating social media pages to build a brand for your business, you can also use them as a resource to find carriers.

You can make regular posts, including articles, videos, reels, and stories, and post them on Facebook, Instagram, Twitter, and LinkedIn pages. Ultimately, this will help you build an online presence and connections with new carriers, owner-operators, and drivers from different parts of your country.

- **Create video ads**

You can also use Facebook and Instagram video ads to promote your dispatching services. For instance, if you are a dispatch company or a dispatch business in Memphis, Tennessee, and you don't want to move a load beyond that area, you can make a video ad that goes like the one below:

"Hey, this is Joe from GoodDispatcher company, and I'm looking for drivers in Memphis, Nashville, Knoxville, etc. If you're interested in making X dollars and are cool with being on the road anytime, I've got a great offer for you. Don't get robbed by these asset-based carriers; they only care about their own profit, not yours. But I'm right here to ensure you get paid and well. So don't hesitate to hit me up."

A video ad like this will show you know what you're doing and are different from others.

Join Facebook trucking and dispatching groups

When you join these groups, you want to ensure that you are actively commenting and creating posts so that people can notice you.

Owner-operators and drivers are always in these groups reading posts and comments and interacting. So you want to leverage this opportunity to promote your business, especially since it's free.

- **Email lists**

You should create a mailing list and promote your business to them. Let subscribers know what you're doing at the moment, whether it's a unique offering, a discount code for the Christmas season, or just a black holiday offer. You want to keep your name in their ears always, and here are three ways I recommend you build your email list:

Create a newsletter and add it to your website for people to see and subscribe to it. Remember, you want genuine subscriptions for your email list; in other words, only those who are interested in your services should be on your list. That way, you don't go about spamming people and sending emails to those who aren't interested in what you do.

If you couldn't work for a carrier on your first attempt, you can ask them to permit you to send regular emails for your next available offer. If they agree, then you can add them to your mailing list. But ensure you ask them first so that they won't mark your emails as spam when they receive them later.

You can use your dispatcher service agreement, which will work effectively for your existing customers. Under your dispatcher service agreement, you can have a column where you ask for their permission to receive promotional offers from time to time via email. If they check yes, you can add them manually to your email lists and start sending them your emails for future offers.

2. **Offline Methods of Finding a Carrier**

- **Utilizing truck stops**

If you're at a truck stop, like a gas station, you can go outside to check other drivers. You want to know if they're driving for a big or small company. And one way to do this is to check the signs on their truck because trucks for big companies, like JB Hunt, will have their name written on the truck.

Trucks for small companies usually do not have signs; if they do, they'll likely have random names you've never heard of before. And it's the drivers of such trucks you want to meet and communicate with to know which carrier or owner-operators they're working for. That way, you can go on to develop a good working relationship for your future shipments.

- **Networking**

Again, you can't downplay the huge role networking plays in the trucking industry. You'll have to network with other dispatchers, brokers, carriers, owner-operators, and family and friends.

Yes, family and friends are essential because, one way or the other, someone knows someone who is a driver, a carrier, or an owner-operator who is either working for themselves or working for a company. So don't hesitate to tighten up your networking game.

- **Cold Calling**

When it comes to cold calling, you want to pay attention to how you talk to carriers and what to expect. So I've shared three tactics you can use, but remember you're doing sales calls when cold calling.

The first tactic is to have a long introduction so that when you call the carrier, you'll be able to introduce yourself properly. Here's an example:

"Hi, my name is Jane. I'm from Freight Logistics, and I work as an independent dispatcher. I find loads for carriers and owner-operators carriers, so just tell me where you want to go, and I'll handle it for a small fee."

In the second tactic, you go straight to the point. You call a carrier, and you tell them . . .

"Hi, my name is Jane. I'm from Freight Logistics and can help you find loads immediately. So just tell me your current location and where you would like to go."

You see, that's straight to the point because you don't want to waste their time.

The third tactic, which is my favorite, is to call the carrier or owner-operator and quickly introduce yourself. Something like . . .

"Hi, my name is Jane, and I'm from Freight Logistics. I see you have a truck posted, and you're looking to go to Michigan. Do you need a load to haul?"

(You wait for them to say yes, and then you continue)

That's great! I can find you a load, so tell me what exactly you need: the weight, the pickup and delivery times, and your ideal rate, and I'll start working on it immediately."

And then you tell them to give you five minutes to work on it and get back to them. Sometimes, the carrier may say they aren't interested. But that's when you want to tell them about your introductory front-end offers and see if they'll like them. And if they hesitate further, you can note down their name, phone number, and the conversation you had with them, and then add them to your email list and follow them up later.

To make the task of cold-calling easy for you, **I've also created a spreadsheet for collecting cold-calling data. It's available as a sub-sheet in—All-in-One Dispatch**

Management Spreadsheet.

Remember to talk about your USP when pitching your introductory front-end offers to them. You also have to be sound, reliable, and trustworthy for them to work with you. You don't want to be too polite but be professional and respectful.

In this next section, I'll share the scripts I use to call and close carriers, so just hang on.

- **Bulk text messages**

Instead of texting carriers and drivers individually to tell them about your services and any current special offers you may have, you should send them text messages in bulk using apps like Text Magic, Textedly, and EZ Texting.

- **Magic formula**

The shocking truth is there isn't any magic formula anywhere regarding finding new carriers. The success rate of all the work you do, the actions you take, and the way you think all comes down to your persistence. If you aren't persistent in all you do, then I'm sorry to tell you that you'll accomplish nothing. It's the truth. If you look at those big companies, you'll find that none of them made it overnight. It's a series of hard work put together over the years that have brought them to where they are currently. So you've got to stay focused and be persistent in everything you do.

Scripts to Use When Calling Carriers

Believe it or not, it would be best to use a script when calling carriers to help you win over at least one out of every ten carriers. Of course, you have to craft the script incredibly well so that the carrier has no choice but to say yes!

Before we proceed, I'd love to share an illustration to show you why you need to use a script when cold-calling.

For instance, let's say you can call fifty carriers every day and close only one in the end. So in one week, you can close at least five carriers.

Let's say you find a load for one carrier and proceed with the dispatching process. Averagely, most trucks travel 65 miles per hour and about 750 miles a day. And the average pay is around $2 per mile. So this means the carrier will earn an average of $1,500, right?

Assuming you charge your carrier a 10% fee, you'll get $150. And if that carrier can run the truck at least three times a week, that leaves you a total earning of $450.

But recall I said you could close at least five carriers per week; that means you'll earn a total of $2,250 per week, which equals $117,000 in one year (52 weeks). That's a whopping sum of money, showing that earning a six-figure income with truck dispatching is possible.

Now, I don't want you to do all the hard work, so **I have put together the killer scripts I use to close carriers. Check out the Free Bonus #13 to get your copy. All you need to do is to review & edit to apply them in your dispatching business.**

How to Keep Your Carriers

Do you recall the old saying, "You can't please everyone all of the time"? If you work in the trucking industry, where maintaining client satisfaction is one of the fundamental business principles, you may want to reevaluate that statement.

I understand that pleasing people takes effort. But you've got to press on to ensure that your carriers are satisfied, steadfast in their support of your business, and continue to put their trust in you. So here are the things you want to do:

- **Have good customer relations**

Yes, you should have good customer relations and develop great relationships with your carriers. Answer their calls whenever they call, find them a load whenever they need one, offer them help, and point them in the right direction whenever they ask for it. Go above and beyond to make things work and respect their wishes.

- **Have finder's rewards**

One of the best parts of the dispatching business is when a carrier advocates for you—when they tell their friends, drivers, and other owner-operators or carrier companies that they've got this great dispatcher, which is you. Isn't that awesome? But you know, you've got to compensate them for that. You can offer any carrier who refers new clients to you a discount, a special offer, or small cash you can afford; it's something I call the finder's reward. That way, they'll feel led to do even more.

- **Use word-of-mouth**

You see, succeeding as a dispatcher isn't just about finding carriers and drivers; you've got to fight to keep them. And keeping them is good, but what's better is having them look for other drivers for you. If you're using a good carrier service, you'll usually want to recommend them to your colleagues. It's the same way with those you work with. When you offer them exceptional services, and they're happy with you, they'll go all the way to talk about you and recommend your business to others. That's how word-of-mouth marketing works in the trucking industry. Ultimately, you'll get more new customers and make more money without spending on advertisements.

Wrapping up, I would say the period of scaling your business is when you need to shift your mind from playing the solo game to building a dependable business. It's when you establish your core values, define your company's culture and brand identity, and develop plans to expand your market reach.

I admit it's not an easy thing to do, but this is why you must do it as thoughtfully and carefully as possible. The topic of "scaling your business" is the make-or-break discussion of your dispatching business. Marketing and networking are where you need to shine to scale your business fast and grow a visible brand. So always make sure you do your homework.

Key Takeaway

1. As a small dispatching business, you may compete against big trucking players with devoted clients and substantial marketing budgets. So you must find ways to build your brand and make it stand out from the crowd.

2. You can leverage various online and offline methods to find carriers. Online methods include load boards, trucking authority directories, job boards, social media, etc. In contrast, offline methods include truck stops, networking, cold calling, etc.

3. While it may be a daunting task to please your carriers, you've got to press on to ensure that they're satisfied, steadfast in their support of your business, and continue to put their trust in you.

Conclusion

"What do you need to start a business? Three simple things: know your product better than anyone, know your customer, and have a burning desire to succeed."

— Dave Thomas

Truck dispatching introduces you to a new world of experiences and offers immense opportunities for you to make money in the trucking industry. In addition, meeting new people from around the world is another one of the many incredible advantages of working as an independent dispatcher.

Luckily, this *Freight Dispatcher Training* guide can help you make the whole setup process a breeze. It's the perfect roadmap if you want to do the freight dispatch business the right way and start making six figures. Although the job is demanding since you'll likely be dealing with frequent calls and emails from your clients and truck drivers, with the strategies we have covered in this book, you'll be able to stay organized and be at the top of your game. So what's next?

Well, what's next is for you to go out there and start taking actionable steps toward setting up your business! You already have all the tools, so just go out there and use them.

It would also mean a great deal to me if you could take the time to leave a review on Amazon about the book. Positive reviews from wonderful customers like you help others feel confident about choosing the *Freight Dispatcher Training* Book. Sharing your positive experience will be greatly appreciated!

If the techniques shared in the book helped you, then kindly also tell your friends and colleagues about it.

I wish you the very best in your truck-dispatching journey!

To your success,

Kayla Hobson

REFERENCES

Alfa X Logistics. (2022, February 7). *Should you use a dispatch service agreement?* https://www.youtube.com/watch?v=a9Vad4S5Xho

Alfa X Logistics. (2020, November 5). *Two must-have skills for every truck dispatcher.* https://www.youtube.com/watch?v=JddcjKEJsJk&t=120s

Alfa X Logistics. (2020, November 10). *Learn how truck dispatchers get paid.* https://www.youtube.com/watch?v=v0DnGcdJIZM&t=191s

Aljex. (2015). *ALJEX list.* http://www.aljex.com/wp-content/uploads/2015/06/Equipment-Type-Definitions.pdf

Altexsoft Blog. (2022, June 7). *Load boards for trucking: functionality overview, integration options, and top players comparison.* https://www.altexsoft.com/blog/load-boards

Brandon Manney The Mentor. (2022, March 9). *Freight broker vs dispatcher what is the big difference? Which one do you want to start, choose?* https://www.youtube.com/watch?v=KHGjQ76yIbk&t=71s

Bumble Bee Dispatch. (2018, February 4). *Freight dispatcher training how to fill out a carrier packet for trucking company.* https://www.youtube.com/watch?v=_i9YnwfMloU

DAT. (2021). *DAT list.* https://www.dat.com/wp-content/uploads/2021/02/postsearchreference.pdf

Diamonds In The Ruff Logistics, LLC. (2021, November 15). *Trucking business: how to get started dispatching?* https://www.youtube.com/watch?v=oEX-6j3Sq5o&t=132s

Diamonds In The Ruff Logistics, LLC. (2021, November 17). Trucking terminology that every truck dispatcher must know. https://www.youtube.com/watch?v=NAsM2Fabkz8&t=234s

Diamonds In The Ruff Logistics, LLC. (2021, November 27). Trucking business: how to properly book a load! https://www.youtube.com/watch?v=idUwz6J-jCg&t=377s

Diamonds In The Ruff Logistics, LLC. (2022, January 19). Trucking business: how to become a dispatcher, pros and cons, marketing & networking. Must watch. https://www.youtube.com/watch?v=Z5Xkc7eqEUc&t=835s

Diamonds In The Ruff Logistics, LLC. (2022, June 15). Let's talk about load boards! Part one. https://www.youtube.com/watch?v=Cxvq84oIsZ0&t=104s

Dispatch Trucks. (2019, March 19). Learning the key players: what/who is a shipper? How to become a truck dispatcher part 2 of 9. https://www.youtube.com/watch?v=Wl0HKSc90SA

Dispatch Trucks. (2019, March 22). Freight industry: what is factoring? how to become a truck dispatcher part 6 of 9. https://www.youtube.com/watch?v=2BRTO1hJeAc

Dispatch Trucks. (2019, November 14). How paperwork process works to get paid in 2022 truck dispatcher training. https://www.youtube.com/watch?v=5lgPYl45VG8

Dispatch Trucks. (2022, January 18). Load board training— what you need to know in 2022. https://www.youtube.com/watch?v=0DOy2ydjHQ0&t=4414s

Good Energy Worldwide. (2021, May 6). Trucking business— the difference between dispatcher & freight broker https://www.youtube.com/watch?v=nWs_NNzpEyI&t=11s

Is Being A Truck Dispatcher Worth It? (2021, September 21). Is being a truck dispatcher stressful? https://www.youtube.com/watch?v=b3AgRJJNUwc

Makhmudov, K. (2021). *Startup guide: how to become a truck dispatcher.* https://www.dat.com/resources/how-to-become-a-truck-dispatcher

Motive Blog. (2018, October 23). How much does it cost to start a trucking company? https://gomotive.com/blog/cost-starting-trucking-business

Never Stop Trucking. (2021, November 12). How should a truck dispatcher plan a trip based on the route and driver's hos. https://www.youtube.com/watch?v=ft5avoI2mRU&t=1327s

Never Stop Trucking. (2021, December 23). Which are the best and worst areas to send your trucks to? https://www.youtube.com/watch?v=NcerCKFgqYg

Never Stop Trucking. (2022, January 24). How to find owner operators as a dispatcher—the ultimate guide. https://www.youtube.com/watch?v=r0S8YcfSeHA&t=2628s

PorterFreight. (2021). Common types of trucking equipment. https://www.porterfreightfunding.com/2021/10/14/different-types-of-equipment-dispatch-in-trucking/

RBBS Logistics Learning Center. (2021, February 10). How 2 dispatch training dispatch agreement & carrier profile form. https://www.youtube.com/watch?v=wDQyi8KN47c&t=2576s

wikiHow Staff. (2022, July 28). How to become a truck dispatcher. https://www.wikihow.com/Become-a-Truck-Dispatcher

Made in the USA
Monee, IL
22 January 2023